HODDER GEOGRAPHY

Series Editor: JEFF BATTERSBY Series Consultant: ROBERT PROSSER

RIVERS &
COASTS

Andrew John

Hodder & Stoughton

A MEMBER OF THE HODDER HEADLINE GROUP

Acknowledgements

The author wishes to express his thanks to his family for their support – Jane, Kieran and Eleanor. This book is for them.

Cover photo from Telegraph Colour Library.

Orders queries: please contact Bookpoint Ltd, 39 Milton Park, Abingdon, Oxon OX14 4TD. Telephone: (44) 01235 400414, Fax: (44) 01235 400454. Lines are open from 9.00–6.00, Monday to Saturday, with a 24 hour message answering service. Email address: orders@bookpoint.co.uk

British Library Cataloguing in Publication Data
A catalogue record for this title is available from The British Library

ISBN 0 340 70196 X

First published 1998
Impression number   10 9 8 7 6 5 4 3 2
Year   2003 2002 2001 2000 1999 1998

Copyright © 1998 Andrew John

Typeset by Wearset, Boldon, Tyne and Wear.
Printed in Hong Kong for Hodder & Stoughton Educational, a division of Hodder Headline Plc, 338 Euston Road, London NW1 3BH by Colorcraft Ltd.

CONTENTS

Chapter 1

River Landforms   **Pages 1–15**

Chapter 2

Rivers in flood   **Pages 16–24**

Chapter 3

Coastal landforms   **Pages 25–33**

Chapter 4

Cliff collapse   **Pages 34–46**

Chapter 5

Coastal flooding   **Pages 47–60**

Glossary

abrasion scraping action of materials transported in rivers

alluvium the sediment deposited by a river

attrition when loose material collides and breaks into smaller pieces

backwash waves that move eroded material down a beach

cliffs high/steep rock faces

coast narrow area between the land and the sea

coastal system processes by which coasts are formed

condensation processes by which droplets are formed when vapour is cooled

confluence the point where a tributary joins main channel

corrosion when rocks are dissolved in water

cross-profile landform viewed from one side to another

deltas landform produced by the deposition of sediment at river mouth

deposition laying down of sediment on the bed of a river

depressions huge areas of low atmospheric pressure

drainage basin catchment area from which a river obtains its supplies of water

ebb tidal fall

Environmental Agency body responsible for controlling the flood hazard; also called EA

evaporation process by which liquid becomes vapour

fetch the length of open sea over which a wind blows to generate waves

flood river/tidal rise

flood hazard the threat of flooding

flood plain part of a valley floor which a river may flood

freeze/thaw form of mechanical weathering

global warming gradual warming of the Earth's atmosphere

groundwater water which collects underground in the pore spaces in soil and rock

headlands coastal promontory resulting from the existence of more resistant rock

hydraulic action the force of moving water

hydroelectric power energy created by water flowing through turbines

hydrological cycle circulation of water

landforms distinctive coastal areas produced by erosional processes

landslides movement of debris down high/steep inclines

levees small embankments

long-profile view of a landform from source to mouth

meanders bends in a river

Ox-bow lakes cut–off lakes

polders land reclaimed from the sea for farming

precipitation water in any form that falls from the atmosphere to the surface of the Earth

relief shape of the landscape

ria formed when a river valley reaching the sea becomes drowned

saltation when smaller stones are bounced along the river bed

salt marsh develop in the sheltered waters behind the spit

sand dunes develop when winds pick up sands from the spit

source the point at which a stream begins

storm surge depressions cause the surface of the sea to rise and push the increased water levels towards land

surface run-off water that returns to the sea through rivers

swash waves that move eroded material up a beach

traction when rock is swept along the river bed by gravity

transportation movement of materials in a river

tributary streams that lead into rivers

tropical cyclones intense depressions

tsunamis large tidal waves

watershed an area of high ground which divides two river systems

water table level below the surface of the ground where water can be found

wave-cut notch formed at the base of a cliff as a result of erosional processes

wave cut platform gently sloping rock surface caused by cliff retreat due to the erosional actions of the sea

RIVER LANDFORMS

Key Idea

Water is constantly moving around the earth and its atmosphere. This can be in the hydrological cycle, in weather, in seas or in rivers. This movement of water causes great changes to landforms which in turn affect the people that live there. This chapter looks at the different ways water affects the earth.

What is the Hydrological (Water) Cycle?

The circulation of water from the oceans to the atmosphere, to the land and back to the oceans is called the Water Cycle or **Hydrological Cycle**. Hydrology is the study of water. The cycle involves several processes. When the ocean is warmed up by the sun, some **evaporation** may occur resulting in water changing from the liquid into a vapour. Air containing the water vapour rises from the earth's surface, expands and is cooled into drops of water. This is called **condensation**. The water falls to earth in either liquid or solid form as **precipitation** (the collective word for rain, sleet, snow and hail). It is then either stored as ice (in glaciers), water (in lakes and in the soil) or returned to the oceans and seas. Most water returns to the sea through rivers as **surface run-off**. The rest returns as **groundwater** through the soil and rocks below the **Water Table**. The water table is the level below the surface of the ground where water can be found. Further evaporation may occur from vegetation, the soil, lakes and rivers back into the atmosphere. These processes and links within the cycle are shown in Resource 1.1.

RESOURCE 1.1
The processes and links within the Hydrological Cycle

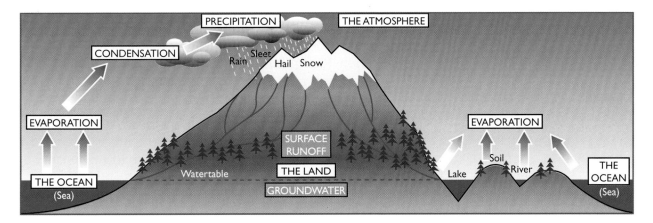

What is a Drainage (River) Basin?

When water falls on an area of land as precipitation it can either run off the surface or flow through the soil into the rock beneath. Eventually through one of these methods it will arrive at a river or the sea. The area of land whose water runs into this river is known as the **drainage basin**.

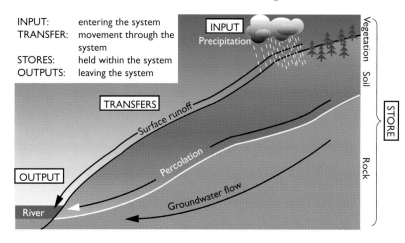

INPUT: entering the system
TRANSFER: movement through the system
STORES: held within the system
OUTPUTS: leaving the system

RESOURCE 1.2
The drainage basin as a system of inputs, transfers, stores and outputs

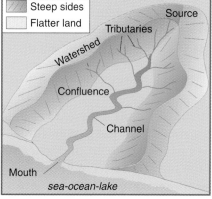
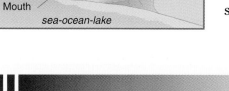

Steep sides
Flatter land

RESOURCE 1.3
The main features of a drainage basin

The movement of water is called a transfer. When water is not moving it can be stored in lakes, soil, rock and vegetation. Eventually the water is either carried to the oceans or seas or evaporates from lakes, soil and vegetation on sunny days. These are outputs. This is shown in Resource 1.2.

Following rainfall, water will often collect and flow in a channel forming a small stream on the surface. The point at which the stream begins is called its **source**. As it continues downhill it will be joined by other streams, called **tributaries**. The point where a tributary joins the main channel is called the **confluence**. The main channel or river eventually flows into a sea, ocean or lake. This is the river's mouth. This is shown in Resource 1.3.

1. What is the Hydrological Cycle?

2. Using Resource 1.1 draw a labelled diagram to show the hydrological cycle using the following terms: Evaporation, Condensation, Precipitation and Surface Runoff.

3. Describe and explain how the Hydrological Cycle works.

4. What is a Drainage Basin?

5. Resource 1.4 shows the drainage basin of the River Glaven, Norfolk. Match up the letters (A–F) with the following terms: Source, Channel, Tributary, Confluence, Mouth and Watershed.

How do natural drainage basins differ?

All drainage basins are bordered by a **watershed**, (an area of high ground which divides two river systems), and collect water from a wide area, but no two are exactly the same. Basins may differ for a variety of reasons. These include – their size and shape; the number and size of tributaries; the shape of the landscape (**the relief**); the soil and rock type; the vegetation cover and climate type.

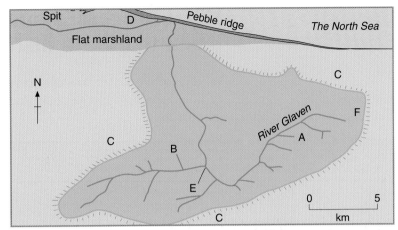

RESOURCE 1.4 River Glaven, Norfolk

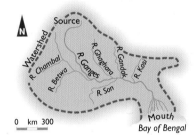

RESOURCE 1.5 River Ganges, Asia

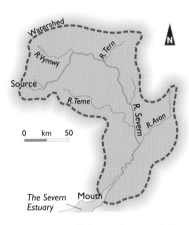

RESOURCE 1.6 River Severn, UK

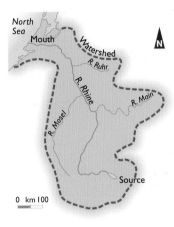

RESOURCE 1.7 River Rhine, Europe

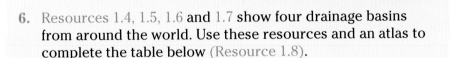

6. Resources 1.4, 1.5, 1.6 and 1.7 show four drainage basins from around the world. Use these resources and an atlas to complete the table below (Resource 1.8).

RESOURCE 1.8
The drainage basin features of the rivers Glaven, Severn, Rhine and Ganges

Feature	Drainage Basin			
	Glaven	Severn	Rhine	Ganges
Location				
Size of basin				
Number of tributaries				
Height of ground near source				
Name of ocean/sea at mouth				
Soil/rock/vegetation cover				
Climate – rainfall (mm) – temperature (°C)				
Other features				

What processes operate in a drainage basin to create distinctive landforms?

When surface water in a drainage basin flows over the land it can erode, transport and deposit material to create distinctive landforms.

RESOURCE 1.9
The 4 processes of erosion

Term	River
Attrition	Fragments break off — Movement of material
Abrasion (or Corrasion)	Sandpapering effect — Bank
Corrosion	Bubbles of gas
Hydraulic action	Fast flowing river — Bank

Term	River
Traction	
Saltation	Leap-frogging action
Suspension	Brown colouration
Solution	

RESOURCE 1.10
The 4 processes of transportation

THE PROCESSES OF EROSION

There are four main processes by which a river can change the landscape. **Hydraulic action** refers to the force of moving water which is able to break off bits of solid rock by repeatedly flowing into cracks. **Abrasion** occurs when the loose material carried by the river is thrown against the sides of the river (the banks) and pushed along the bed (floor). **Attrition** occurs as the loose material collides and breaks up into smaller pieces. **Corrosion** or solution occur when rocks are dissolved into the water (Resource 1.9).

THE PROCESSES OF TRANSPORTATION

Transportation or movement of material by a river occurs in four ways. **Solution** occurs as dissolved material is carried in suspension. **Traction** occurs when rock fragments, stones and even boulders are rolled along the river bed by gravity and the force of the flowing water. Whereas, **saltation** occurs when smaller stones are bounced along the bed in a leap frogging manner (Resource 1.10).

THE PROCESSES OF DEPOSITION

Deposition takes place when a river has insufficient flow to transport all the material it is carrying so it drops some. The larger rock fragments are dropped first due to their weight, whereas the finer materials are deposited later.

What landforms are found in river valleys?

River processes form a series of landforms and although no two river valleys are alike, many show similar **long-profile** (from source to mouth) and **cross-profile** (across the valley) characteristics (Resource 1.11).

In the upper section of a river, water collects in streams and rivers on the steep slopes of the land. Because the river flow is fast down the slopes, the water and eroded material are powerful agents of erosion, carving out an easily recognisable **V-shaped valley**. The river flows from side to side due to a natural tendency and because of obstacles, like hard rock, to form **inter-locking spurs**. **Waterfalls** and **rapids** are also formed due to the wearing down of different rock hardness. A **gorge** might also be formed.

In the middle section, the river no longer has the speed to cut vertically as it did in the upper section. It still, however, has enough speed to grind the material which it is transporting against the river's banks and in this way it begins to cut sideways into the valley slopes to widen the valley floor. Where the river's side-to-side movement was causing inter-locking spurs, now that it is flatter it causes **meanders**, or bends in the river. Deposition begins to take place mainly along the inside of meanders. Deposition also occurs right across the valley floor, as the river level goes down after it has been in flood. The deposited material or **alluvium** forms the **flood plain**. As the meanders move across the flood plain, they leave stretches which are never worn down by the river, called **terraces**.

RESOURCE 1.11
Long profile and cross profile characteristics of a river valley

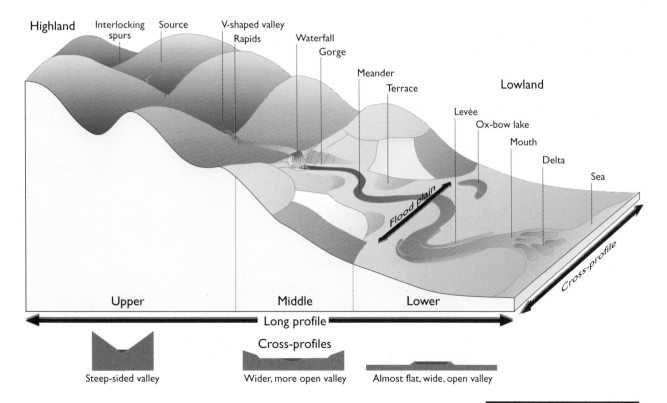

RESOURCE 1.12
Landforms in a river valley

In the lower section, there is an almost flat, wide open valley and a wider flood plain. Cut-off lakes or **ox-bow lakes** form where the meander has worn away one side of its bend and deposited material at the other side until eventually the two bends meet, the river joins up and leaves the original meander as an ox-bow lake. The river banks are built up by repeated flooding to form raised levees. When the river reaches the mouth, flow is at its slowest, so deposition is greatest and a **delta** may be formed.

7. What do the following terms mean?

   Hydraulic action   Attrition

   Abrasion   Solution

8. How does a river transport material? Draw diagrams to help your explanation.

9. **a)** Resource 1.12 is a simplified drawing of the landforms in a river valley. Make a copy of the drawing.

   b) Add the terms below to the drawing in the correct places. Resource 1.11 will help you.

   Upper section landforms

      V-shaped valley   Waterfall

      Interlocking spurs   Rapids

   Middle and lower section landforms

      Meander   Ox-bow lake

      Flood plain   Levee

      Terrace   Delta

How do river and weathering processes create landforms in highland areas?

RESOURCE 1.13
Landforms created by weathering and river processes near the source of the River Severn, highland Wales

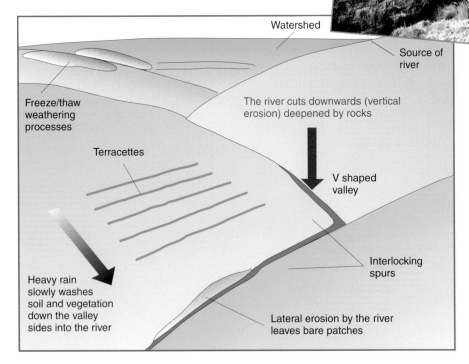

Watershed

Source of river

Freeze/thaw weathering processes

The river cuts downwards (vertical erosion) deepened by rocks

Terracettes

V shaped valley

Interlocking spurs

Heavy rain slowly washes soil and vegetation down the valley sides into the river

Lateral erosion by the river leaves bare patches

RESOURCE 1.14 Photo showing source area of the River Severn showing V-shaped valley and interlocking spurs

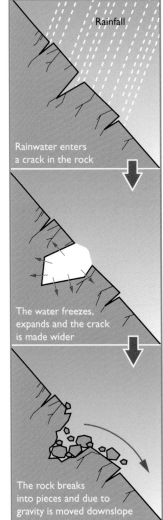

Rainfall

Rainwater enters a crack in the rock

The water freezes, expands and the crack is made wider

The rock breaks into pieces and due to gravity is moved downslope

RESOURCE 1.15 Freeze/thaw weathering processes

One of the most significant forms of weathering processes (when rocks are attacked by the weather), is a process known as **freeze/thaw** (Resource 1.13). There are clear examples of this near to Plynlimon, the source area of the River Severn in the Cambrian Mountains of Wales (Resources 1.14 and 1.15). Rainwater collects in the cracks in the rocks. If it freezes and turns to ice, the water expands and exerts considerable pressure on the surrounding rocks. When it thaws, the ice melts and changes back to water, leaving behind small fragments of rock which have been broken off. When repeated, this process weakens the rock considerably, leaving fragments to be transported down the valley sides due to gravity. Biological weathering occurs when burrowing and grazing animals disturb the soil and vegetation and expose more rock to freeze/thaw weathering. After periods of heavy rain the weathered material slowly moves downhill to form **terracettes**.

When the weathered stones and rocks reach the river, they scrape along the river bed, eroding downwards. Continued weathering weakens the banks of the river channel as the loose rock and soil washes down the sides. Although lateral erosion like this does take place, the deepening or downcutting processes dominate in highland areas.

RAPIDS, WATERFALLS AND GORGES

Rapids, waterfalls and gorges often form where a river, having flowed across hard resistant rock flows across softer, less resistant rock. Rapids and small waterfalls (Resource 1.16) are formed when there is a small change in slope due to changes in rock hardness, whereas larger waterfalls (Resource 1.17) are formed due to much greater changes of slope and rock hardness. The river flows over the hard resistant rock, and erodes the soft rock that it comes to. Gradually a deep lake called a plunge pool is created (stage 1). The river continues to erode the softer rock leaving the hard rock above unsupported, which leads to collapse (stage 2). Over time the waterfall moves backwards (stage 3) and may develop a gorge (stage 4). One of the most famous waterfalls and gorge is at Niagara, on the Canada/USA border (Resource 1.17).

RESOURCE 1.16
How rapids and small waterfalls are formed

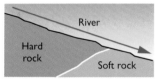

As the river flows over the harder rock it comes in contact with the softer rock. The softer rock is less resistant to the rivers' erosive powers and so is worn away more quickly

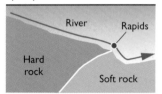

A step is produced at the edge of the hard rock and rapids are created, as more softer rock is eroded and transported by the river

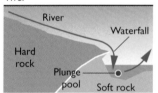

Increased erosion undermines the front of the hard rock. The overhang collapses due to gravity, leaving a sharp drop creating a waterfall

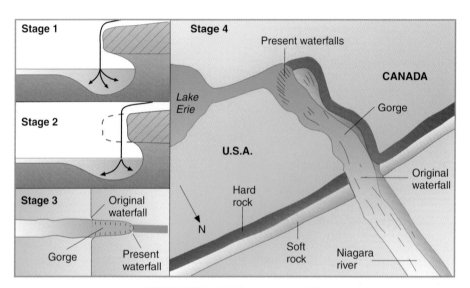

RESOURCE 1.17 How a waterfall changes to create a gorge

10. Describe what weathering is. Name two processes. (Use Resource 1.13)

11. Using Resources 1.15, 1.16 and 1.17, draw clearly labelled diagrams to describe and explain how the following landforms have been formed:

   V-shaped Valley and Interlocking Spurs

   Rapids

   Waterfall and Gorge

12. Describe and explain why rock type and weathering processes are important in landform development.

How do river processes create landforms in lowland areas?

MEANDERS AND OX-BOW LAKES

A river tends naturally to swing from side to side and the bends that develop are known as meanders (Resource 1.18). Think about when you go too fast around a corner on a bicycle, you have to learn to lean over to stop falling off. In fact, if you are going too fast and do not lean over enough, or if you lean over too far, you will slide off and crash. This idea can be applied to meanders. When the river water swings round a bend it will not, of course, be able to lean over and so it will crash into the outside bend. Since it is carrying its load, it will continually wear away the outside of the bend, while the inside bend will be an area of calmer water in which mud and sand will tend to collect (Resource 1.19). Ox-bow lakes are formed when the river cuts through the neck of land separating two meanders. The original meander is then blocked off leaving an ox-bow lake (Resource 1.20).

RESOURCE 1.18
Meanders along the River Severn

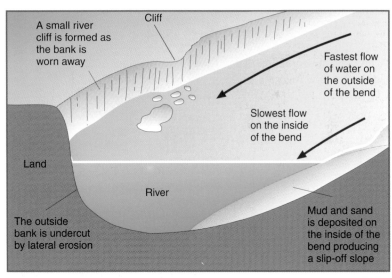

RESOURCE 1.19
Cross-section of a meander

A small river cliff is formed as the bank is worn away

Cliff

Fastest flow of water on the outside of the bend

Slowest flow on the inside of the bend

Land

River

The outside bank is undercut by lateral erosion

Mud and sand is deposited on the inside of the bend producing a slip-off slope

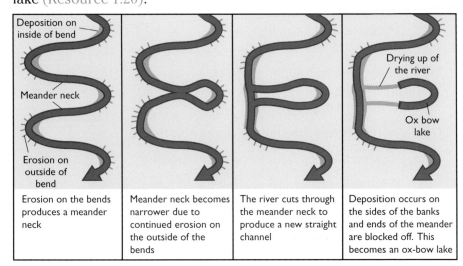

Deposition on inside of bend

Meander neck

Erosion on outside of bend

			Drying up of the river
			Ox bow lake
Erosion on the bends produces a meander neck	Meander neck becomes narrower due to continued erosion on the outside of the bends	The river cuts through the meander neck to produce a new straight channel	Deposition occurs on the sides of the banks and ends of the meander are blocked off. This becomes an ox-bow lake

RESOURCE 1.20
Four stage formation of an ox-bow lake

FLOOD PLAINS AND LEVEES

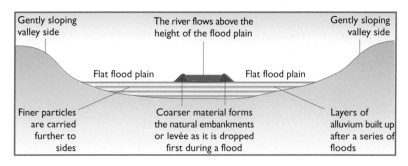

Gently sloping valley side

The river flows above the height of the flood plain

Gently sloping valley side

Flat flood plain   Flat flood plain

Finer particles are carried further to sides

Coarser material forms the natural embankments or levée as it is dropped first during a flood

Layers of alluvium built up after a series of floods

RESOURCE 1.21
Cross-section of a lowland valley showing the flood plain and levees

RESOURCE 1.22
Bangladesh and its large delta

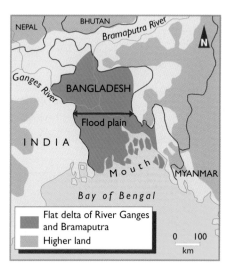

NEPAL

BHUTAN

Bramaputra River

N

Ganges River

BANGLADESH

Flood plain

INDIA

Mouth

MYANMAR

Bay of Bengal

Flat delta of River Ganges and Bramaputra

Higher land

0   100
km

RESOURCE 1.23
Incomplete cross-section of a meander on the River Glaven, Norfolk

An area of flat land develops beside the meandering river. This is liable to be flooded during times of high rainfall, when fine material or alluvium is deposited over the flooded area. This area is called the flood plain. Heavier material is deposited closer to the river and forms small embankments or **levees** (Resource 1.21).

Deltas

Deltas are formed at the mouth of a river due to the deposition of large amounts of alluvium. This is because as a river flows into a larger mass of water (sea or ocean) it will be slowed down and will drop its load. Bangladesh is located on a delta that has been formed by many large rivers including the Ganges (Resource 1.22).

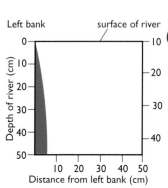

Left bank   surface of river

Depth of river (cm)

Distance from left bank (cm)

Distance from left bank (cm)	Depth of the river (cm)
5	50
10	40
20	30
30	20
40	10
50	0

13. Resource 1.23 is an incomplete cross-section of a meander on the River Glaven, Norfolk.

a) Complete the diagram by using the information given.

b) Add labels in the correct places – fastest flow, slowest flow, deep water, shallow water, erosion and deposition.

c) Give the cross-section a title.

d) Describe and explain how this meander was formed. Use Resource 1.19 to help you.

14. What is likely to happen at Point A, Resource 1.18, in the future? Using Resource 1.20, draw detailed diagrams to describe and explain.

15. Define the terms flood plain, levee and delta.

16. a) How can levees help to prevent flooding?

b) What conditions are needed for a river to form a delta?

What effect can physical processes have on a river channel?

AN ENQUIRY INTO THE WIDTH AND DEPTH OF THE RIVER GLAVEN, NORFOLK.

RESOURCE 1.24
River Glaven and its drainage basin, Norfolk

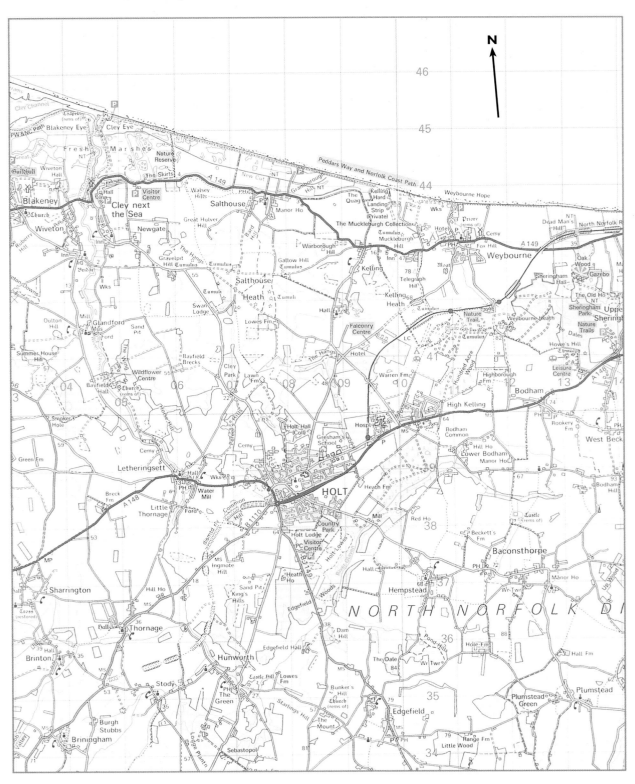

1 km

The River Glaven is one of the finest rivers in a most interesting river valley in North Norfolk (Resource 1.24). The river's source (beginning) is near Bodham (1239) and flows in a south west direction until Hunworth Green (0735) where it turns northwards through the villages of Letheringsett (0539) and Glandford (0441) to flow into the North Sea near Cley (0443). It is a small river, 17 km in length.

A geography fieldwork party collected width and depth measurements at seven locations along the river (Resource 1.25).

RESOURCE 1.25
River channel width and depth measurements

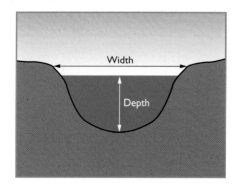

1. Bodham (128392).
2. Alder Carr (114395).
3. Selbrigg Pond (106389).
4. Edgefield Heath (088368)
5. Hunworth Ford (062365).
6. Little Thornage (061384).
7. Glandford (045415).

RESOURCE 1.26
Channel measurements data (width and depth) for seven locations on the River Glaven, Norfolk

The results were tabulated (Resource 1.26).

LOCATION 1	Six Fig Grid. Ref:- 128392		Name of Location:- Bodham			Width of Channel:- 0.20 metres													
Distance across Channel (m)	0.1	0.2																	
Channel Depth (m)	0.04	0.015																	

LOCATION 2	Six Fig Grid. Ref:- 114395		Name of Location:- Alder Carr			Width of Channel:- 1.45 metres													
Distance across Channel (m)	0.2	0.4	0.6	0.8	1	1.2	1.4												
Channel Depth (m)	0.21	0.28	0.23	0.21	0.22	0.20	0.17												

LOCATION 3	Six Fig Grid. Ref:- 106389		Name of Location:- Selbrigg Pond			Width of Channel:- 2.06 metres													
Distance across Channel (m)	0.2	0.4	0.6	0.8	1	1.2	1.4	1.6	1.8	2									
Channel Depth (m)	0.03	0.04	0.05	0.04	0.03	0.03	0.02	0.015	0.014	0.025									

LOCATION 4	Six Fig Grid. Ref:- 088368		Name of Location:- Edgefield Heath			Width of Channel:- 2.6 metres													
Distance across Channel (m)	0.2	0.4	0.6	0.8	1	1.2	1.4	1.6	1.8	2	2.2	2.4							
Channel Depth (m)	0.26	0.33	0.33	0.34	0.34	0.27	0.23	0.14	0.12	0.24	0.10	0.07							

LOCATION 5	Six Fig Grid. Ref:- 062365		Name of Location:- Hunworth Ford			Width of Channel:- 3.95 metres													
Distance across Channel (m)	0.2	0.4	0.6	0.8	1	1.2	1.4	1.6	1.8	2	2.2	2.4	2.6	2.8	3	3.2	3.4	3.6	3.8
Channel Depth (m)	0.045	0.065	0.07	0.068	0.068	0.069	0.065	0.06	0.06	0.06	0.058	0.054	0.055	0.052	0.048	0.048	0.046	0.053	0.034

LOCATION 6	Six Fig Grid. Ref:- 061384		Name of Location:- Little Thornage			Width of Channel:- 8.47 metres													
Distance across Channel (m)	0.5	1	1.5	2	2.5	3	3.5	4	4.5	5	5.5	6	6.5	7	7.5	8			
Channel Depth (m)	0.2	0.22	0.3	0.31	0.39	0.29	0.31	0.3	0.29	0.22	0.28	0.27	0.27	0.21	0.23	0.21			

LOCATION 7	Six Fig Grid. Ref:- 045415		Name of Location:- Glandford			Width of Channel:- 11.5 metres													
Distance across Channel (m)	1	2	3	4	5	6	7	8	9	10	11								
Channel Depth (m)	0.25	0.35	0.45	0.51	0.56	0.59	0.53	0.46	0.42	0.34	0.11								

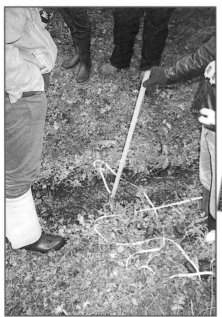

RESOURCE 1.28
Location 5: Hunworth Ford (062365)

RESOURCE 1.27
Location 1: Bodham (128392)

RESOURCE 1.29
Location 7: Glandford (045415)

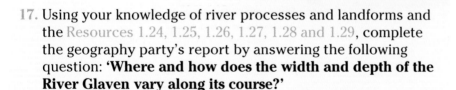

17. Using your knowledge of river processes and landforms and
the Resources 1.24, 1.25, 1.26, 1.27, 1.28 and 1.29, complete
the geography party's report by answering the following
question: **'Where and how does the width and depth of the
River Glaven vary along its course?'**

Your report should contain the following sections:

- **The Question** – simply copy this down.
- **An Introduction** – describe where the river is and
  what it is like.
- **Method** – describe how the width and depth of the
  river was calculated.
- **Results** – draw a cross-section of the river at seven
  locations. Give each cross-section a title, scale and labels.
- **Analysis** – describe the width and depth from location
  1 to location 7. Explain how river processes may have
  changed the river from location 1 to location 7.
- **Conclusion** – answer the question.

How do river processes and landforms affect human activity along the River Severn?

River processes and landforms can affect people in many ways as Resource 1.30 illustrates. The River Severn, Britain's longest river, begins its 354 km journey on the slopes of Plynlimon, in the Cambrian Mountains of Wales (Resource 1.31). The area is a rugged highland region with a climate of cool winters and warm summers. Rainfall is 2500 mm a year on average. The steep V-shaped valleys are used for sheep or hill farming and conifers are often planted. Both are ideally suited to the wet, cold and exposed conditions, some 700 m above sea level. The V-shaped valleys are ideal landforms for creating reservoirs which can be used either as a water supply for homes, industries and farming, or for generating energy, in the form of **hydroelectric power (HEP)**. The highland area provides tourism opportunities, such as absailing, canoeing and hill walking.

As the River Severn flows in a north east direction off the highland areas, it combines with another tributary, the River Vyrnwy, to create a huge flood plain on the border of England and Wales – the Shropshire Plain. Shrewsbury is the first big town located by the river in the flood plain. The river then flows south and eastwards through the narrow Ironbridge Gorge. As the river travels further south, it

RESOURCE 1.30

How river processes and landforms affect human activity

M — Moorland
🌲 — Forestry Commission coniferous plantation
🌳 — Deciduous woodland on steeper slopes
🐑 — Sheepfarming
🐄 — Dairy farming on marshy flood plain
🐄 — Mixed farming on gentler slopes
🚜 — Arable farming on terraces
▓ — Vegetables on drier drained flood plain

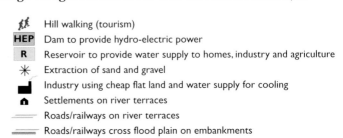

🚶 — Hill walking (tourism)
HEP — Dam to provide hydro-electric power
R — Reservoir to provide water supply to homes, industry and agriculture
✳ — Extraction of sand and gravel
🏭 — Industry using cheap flat land and water supply for cooling
🏠 — Settlements on river terraces
═ — Roads/railways on river terraces
═ — Roads/railways cross flood plain on embankments

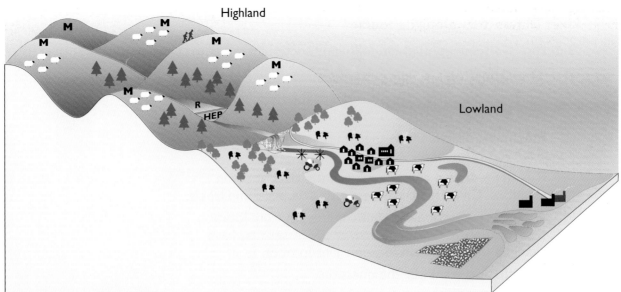

flows over a lowland landscape, having been joined by the Stour, Teme and Avon tributaries. The flood plains are used for grazing dairy cattle. This is because the wet soil makes it difficult to use farm machinery but encourages the growth of thick grass due to the frequent covering of alluvium after flooding, which is a natural fertilizer. The river terraces above the flood plain are drier and so are used for growing crops (arable farming), building roads and railways (communications) and for villages, towns and cities (settlement). Deposited coarse materials of sands and gravels are often used in the construction of homes, industry and for roads and railways.

The gentler sloping valley sides are now used for more mixed farming (rearing animals and growing crops). Deciduous trees are often found on the steeper slopes. Land in the lowest part of the Severn's course is mainly used for rearing animals in the flood plain and vegetable growing on the drier parts. The most intensely farmed area is the Vale of Evesham, where market gardening is highly developed.

Settlements and communications keep to the river terraces or use the embankments on the flood plain to avoid the threat of flooding. The main uses of the river and drainage basin are to supply water for homes (for 6 million people, including the residents of Wolverhampton and Birmingham), industry (the coal fired power station at Ironbridge uses 32 million litres of water a day to help generate electricity) and farming.

RESOURCE 1.31
Generalised land use map of the River Severn's drainage basin

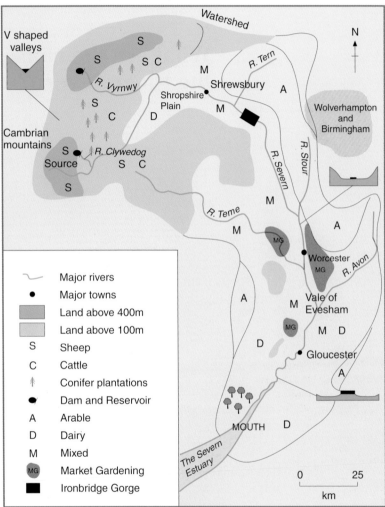

Using Resources 1.30 and 1.31 and an atlas answer the following questions:

18. What is the land use above 400 m, between 400 m and 100 m and below 100 m?

19. Describe and explain how river processes and landforms affect human activity above 400 m, between 400 m and 100 m and below 100 m?

2 RIVERS IN FLOOD

Key Idea

There are many causes and effects of river floods. Equally there are many different options for flood prevention and control.

What are the causes of flooding along the River Severn?

RESOURCE 2.1
The River Severn flooding west of Shrewsbury

A river flood occurs when there is too much water in the river channel, leading to the river overflowing its banks and covering the land. River flooding along the Severn is caused by a combination of physical and human factors. These include:

- **The size and relief of the drainage basin.**

  At 11 400 km², the Severn's basin is the largest in England and Wales and is therefore likely to receive larger amounts of precipitation than a smaller one. In the steep sided, highland valleys, precipitation reaches the river more quickly than in the more gently sloping lowland areas increasing the flood risk.

The type of precipitation.

Near the source, precipitation exceeds 2500 mm a year and winter rainstorms often last for 48 hours. Heavy and prolonged rainfall increases the risk of flooding. During the winter months, heavy snowfall lowers the river levels as water is stored in the snow. However, when temperatures rise in the spring, meltwater will quickly reach the river and so increase the flood risk (Resource 2.2).

Vegetation type.

In the wooded areas, trees intercept precipitation, delay and reduce the amount of water reaching the river. The interception of rainfall is less in grassland and moorland areas due to the low vegetation cover, so the flood risk is increased (Resource 2.3).

Soil type

Clay soils that cover parts of the basin, have tiny pore spaces. Very little rainwater is able to pass through the clay, which increases the flood risk. In some areas sandy soils occur. These have larger pore spaces which allow water to pass through, reducing the flood risk. Flooding may also occur when intense thunderstorms follow a long dry summer period as the soil is hard. Surface runoff is increased leading to a rapid rise in river levels and then flooding.

Number of tributaries.

The higher the number and greater the size of tributaries in a drainage basin, the greater the flow of surface water. As the Severn has twelve large tributaries the flood risk is increased.

High tides.

High tides are when the sea is at its highest level. When this happens, river water has difficulty reaching the sea, increasing the flood risk in the lowland areas.

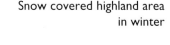

RESOURCE 2.2
Snow covered highland area
in winter

RESOURCE 2.3
The effects of trees and
grasses on rainfall

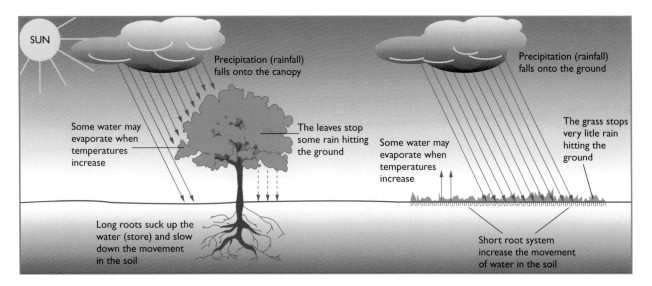

SUN

Precipitation (rainfall) falls onto the canopy

Precipitation (rainfall) falls onto the ground

Some water may evaporate when temperatures increase

The leaves stop some rain hitting the ground

Some water may evaporate when temperatures increase

The grass stops very litle rain hitting the ground

Long roots suck up the water (store) and slow down the movement in the soil

Short root system increase the movement of water in the soil

Human activity.

In urban areas e.g. Gloucester, Worcester and Shrewsbury, impermeable tarmac and concrete surfaces increase the flood risk because the rainwater flows off the surface (Resource 2.4). The risk of flooding can also be increased in deforested areas as there are no trees to intercept and store rainfall, and in farming areas where the soil and water movement is disturbed (e.g. by ploughing).

RESOURCE 2.4
Impermeable tarmac and concrete increase the flood risk

1. What is a river flood?

2. What are the physical and human causes of flooding by the River Severn? Put your answers in a copy of the table below.

Physical Causes	Human Causes

3. Using Resource 2.3, answer the following questions.

    a) What effect does the type of vegetation have on the amount of rainfall reaching the ground surface in the summer?

    b) How will this change in winter?

    c) What might happen if the tree was cut down and the grass ploughed?

4. Why is there a flood risk:

    a) after a summer thunderstorm?

    b) in a highland area with steep slopes, after a period of heavy rainfall?

    c) in an area with an impermeable surface?

5. Using Resource 2.1 and an atlas decide which parts of the Severn's drainage basin are more likely to cause flooding than others. Give reasons for your answers.

What are the effects of flooding by the River Severn?

The effects of flooding include crops lost or damaged and land under water and out of use for long periods of time (Resource 2.1); road and rail routes damaged or lost; the loss of personal property and increased insurance costs. Resource 2.5 illustrates the effect flooding had on the city of Gloucester in February 1995.

RESOURCE 2.5
The effects of flooding by the River Severn on the city of Gloucester, February 1995

GLOUCESTER is still at the mercy of the River Severn today.

Warnings of floods were still in place all day today and river authorities said high tides could again see large areas covered in deep flood water.

Spokesman for the Environment Agency, Steve Branchett, said "In general, the levels we saw yesterday are dropping, but in Gloucester there is still a risk because of the tides. The tide is causing us some concern."

Red warnings also remain in force on the stretch of river including Tewkesbury although indications are that there should be a gradual lowering of levels during the next 24 hours.

Measuring gauges at Epney, Minsterworth and Gloucester showed yesterday morning's tide was lower than anticipated because winds in the Severn estuary had dropped. Another high tide was due at 11am, but again this was expected to be lower than the past two days.

While many residents in areas close to the river were this morning counting the cost of the floods, one Gloucester man was doing his best to help the disabled who might be trapped.

"I am offering a help service to the disabled in the area if they find they need to be moved."

He said that he had already been called by a lady whose house was about to be swamped.

"We were on standby, but the water stopped just an inch from her door so she was alright."

The pub landlord and his wife have evacuated all their animals. Their sons cannot get to school because of the deluge.

But not being able to find an insurance company who will touch the pub, is not so much fun.

One of the regulars at the pub makes the half-mile journey from his cottage up the road in a dinghy he bought at a toy store.

"There was no point sandbagging because my house is 500 years old and the water just comes up through the floor," he said. His lounge and conservatory are now under a foot of water and they may be forced to move out if the water gets any higher.

Read through Resource 2.5 and answer the following questions.

6. What caused the flood to occur?

7. Why wasn't the flooding as bad as had been expected?

8. What were the effects of the floods on:

   a) property?

   b) communications?

   c) people?

9. Why do you think the landlord is unable to find an insurance company to insure the public house from flooding?

10. Imagine you lived in Gloucester during the Great Flood, how would you have responded to the flood threat?

How do people respond to and seek to control the flood hazard?

Flooding by the River Severn is a concern for the people who live and work in the floodplain, the area most at risk. People respond to an attempt to control the flood hazard, in many ways. For example, building reservoirs to hold back the winter flow of water. Clewedog's dam (Resource 2.6) was built when Newtown was severely flooded in 1964 and a flood protection scheme was adopted (Resource 2.7) to reduce the flood risk. Many riverside fields, known as flood meadows, have been allowed to flood to act as overspill reservoirs for flood waters. It is the Environment Agency (EA) which is responsible for controlling the flood hazard. Its work involves the building of flood walls and earth banks. For example, the £25 million scheme between Gloucester and Avonmouth, will give better protection to 8000 people and help to protect 19 000 hectares of farmland (Resource 2.8). The EA also works in conjunction with Local Authorities in seeking to prevent any new development in the flood plain which might be subjected to flooding or which might worsen flooding elsewhere. General maintenance of the river reduces the flood risk. This includes dredging, weed cutting, tree cutting and removing blockages. Finally, the EA provides a Flood Forecasting and Early Warning system using weather forecasts, radar pictures and computer models. All the information provides an accurate forecast so that colour coded warnings (Yellow, Amber and Red) can be issued to the general public, to warn of the severity of the flood (Resource 2.9).

RESOURCE 2.6
Clewedog Reservoir, highland Wales

RESOURCE 2.7
The Severn floods Newtown, 1964 and Newtown Flood Protection Scheme

Key:
- •••••• Bank trimming
- —— Bank trimming and rebuilding
- Concrete river wall
- Earthen embankment
- Roads
- ← Direction of flow

Upstream limit of work

Newly cut straighter river route

N

River Severn

Newtown

Downstream limit of work

Former river course (to be infilled)

0   metres   200

RESOURCE 2.9
The Environment Agency,
formerly the NRA, Flood
Warning System

The three phases of our warning system are:

YELLOW WARNING

Flooding is likely which may affect agricultural land and minor roads. In coastal areas wind blown spray may over-top sea walls. Warnings will identify those areas which are likely to be affected.

AMBER WARNING

Flooding is likely which will affect large areas of agricultural land, roads and isolated properties. Rivers may overtop their banks and waves overtop sea walls. Warnings will be given to identify those areas which may be flooded.

RED WARNING

Flooding is likely and breaching of flood defences and overtopping by rivers is possible. Flooding of commercial and residential property may occur. The NRA will try to give as specific information as possible about which areas are likely to be affected. The NRA has a target for those affected to be warned where practicable two hours before flooding occurs.

If you live or work in an area which is prone to flooding, there will be local arrangements for you to be warned. However you must be ready to take action on receipt of a warning from neighbours, police, local authorities or via the media.

**Action to take if
flood warnings are issued**

● Check your neighbours are aware of the warning and are able to cope.

● Move people, pets and valuables to an upper floor if possible.

● Collect and secure valuables, money, important papers and irreplaceable items such as photograph albums.

● Listen to your local radio station for updates on the situation.

● Have spare warm clothing, waterproofs and wellington boots available.

● Take a torch and a battery powered radio with you.

● Have food which needs no cooking or refrigeration available.

● Switch off the gas and electricity if you are flooded or evacuated.

● Secure items which could float and be damaged.

● Empty fridges and freezers and leave the doors open.

11. List the ways in which people have responded to and sought to control the flood hazard along the River Severn. Did the way the people of Newtown respond to the floods of 1964 differ? (See Resource 2.7.)

12. What evidence is there in the photograph in Resource 2.6, to suggest that the area is suitable for dam construction?

13. Design a poster suitable for younger children to illustrate the action needed if flood warnings are issued. Use Resource 2.9.

Causes, effects and responses to the flooding of the River Ganges

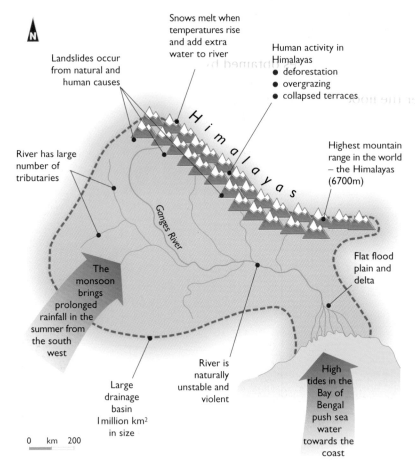

RESOURCE 2.10
Why is the River Ganges prone to flooding?

SOME CAUSES

The River Ganges is a large river in South East Asia. Flooding of the river occurs every year and is caused by a number of factors (Resource 2.10). The Monsoon climate between June and September brings prolonged rainfall (Resource 2.11) which increases the river flow for part of the year. Snowmelt in the Himalayan Mountain Range, near the source, during May and June reaches the delta area by July and overflows onto the flat flood plain. High tides in the Bay of Bengal often prevent the flow of the river reaching the sea. The river is naturally unstable, violent, multi-channelled and is 14 km wide in places. Human activity in the Himalayas, the highest mountain range in the World (6700 m), has resulted in deforestation, overgrazing by animals and collapsed terracing.

This activity has increased erosion, triggered landslides and choked the river and its many tributaries, with transported material. This leads to an increased load and silting of the river in the delta which raises the channel bed and increases the flood risk.

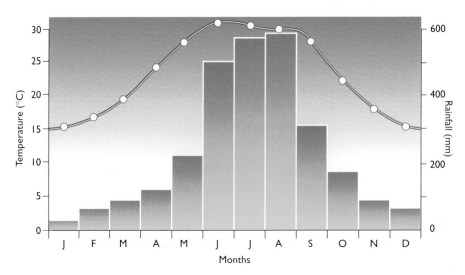

RESOURCE 2.11
Monsoon climate graph for the Ganges Valley

SOME EFFECTS

Severe flooding of the River Ganges occurred in 1984, 1987 and 1988. The latter was a catastrophic flood year in which 2379 people and 172 000 livestock died and 7 million homes were lost or damaged along with 3 million tonnes of rice. In total, the daily lives of 45 million people were affected (Resource 2.12). Other effects include the closure of factories and the loss of monies obtained by selling goods to overseas countries, disruption to roads and railways and a disease hazard after the flooding. In fact more people tend to die from disease than from the flooding itself. Surprisingly, the risk of flooding becomes part of daily life and is regarded as a valuable 'free' water supply and deposited alluvium, a natural fertilizer for growing rice in the paddy fields (Resource 2.13).

RESOURCE 2.12
People clamour for every morsel of food

RESOURCE 2.13
Rice growing in paddy fields

SOME RESPONSES

The Indian Government built the Farakka Dam (Resource 2.14) to divert water from the River Ganges into the River Hooghly. By doing so it succeeded in reducing the flow which has led to an increase in deposited material further down the river in Bangladesh.

Farmers in the Ganges valley welcome floods as fields can be filled with water to grow rice and extra fish can be caught.

After the 1988 Floods, the Flood Action Plan was developed in Bangladesh to protect people and property, to control the water levels, to increase food production and to provide flood warnings and evacuation from flood prone areas into flood shelters. These shelters are also used when cyclones are predicted in the delta area. Opinions on the plan are varied (Resource 2.15).

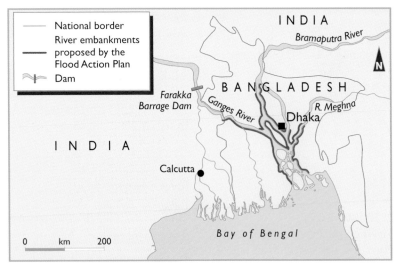

National border

River embankments proposed by the Flood Action Plan

Dam

INDIA
Bramaputra River

BANGLADESH

Farakka
Barrage Dam

Ganges River

R. Meghna

Dhaka

INDIA

Calcutta

0   km   200

Bay of Bengal

RESOURCE 2.14
Responses to flooding

Scientist

If flooding is controlled a new type of rice can be grown. This will produce five times more rice than other types. Millions of people will benefit.

Construction Worker

We have seen, throughout history, that when rivers are controlled or managed, development can take place. Germany and the United States of America are two of the World's richest countries. Managing the Rhine (Germany) and the Mississippi (USA) played a major part in their success! We must develop the plan whatever the cost!

Government Minister

Once people start to 'manage' rivers, they can't stop. Straightening channels and building embankments could increase flooding. This happened in 1993 on the Mississippi. My advice would be 'don't start!'

If embankments are built, we will no longer have our 'free' supply of water for rice and fish stocks will fall. My family and others like us will be forced to move elsewhere to grow and catch food.

Farmer

RESOURCE 2.15
Views on the Flood Action Plan

18. Using Resource 1.8 and an atlas, explain where the River Ganges is and what its drainage basin is like.

19. Why is the river prone to flooding? Use Resources 2.10 and 2.11.

20. What are the positive and negative effects of flooding? Use Resources 2.12 and 2.13.

21. What has been done to try to reduce the flood hazard? Use Resource 2.14.

22. Make a list of those in favour and those against the Flood Action Plan and give reasons for their views. Use Resource 2.15.

23. Make a large copy of the table below to illustrate the causes, effects and human responses to the flooding of the rivers Severn (UK) and Ganges (Asia). Use an atlas and Resources 2.1 to 2.15.

	Causes	Effects	Human Responses
River Severn (UK)			
River Ganges (SE Asia)			

24. In what ways are the causes, effects and human responses

a) the same   b) different?

Suggest reasons why.

COASTAL LANDFORMS

Key Ideas

Distinctive coastal landforms can be found on many different coastlines.

The way they develop depends on a combination of rock type, weathering processes, coastal processes and human activity.

What processes form coastal landforms?

The **coast** is a narrow area between the land and the sea which is constantly changing (Resource 3.1). The three coastal processes are:

- **erosion**
- **transportation**
- **deposition.**

These processes form part of the **coastal system** (Resource 3.2).

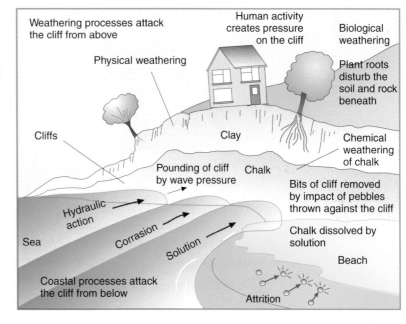

Weathering processes attack the cliff from above

Human activity creates pressure on the cliff

Biological weathering

Physical weathering

Plant roots disturb the soil and rock beneath

Cliffs

Clay

Chemical weathering of chalk

Pounding of cliff by wave pressure

Chalk

Bits of cliff removed by impact of pebbles thrown against the cliff

Hydraulic action

Corrasion

Solution

Chalk dissolved by solution

Sea

Beach

Coastal processes attack the cliff from below

Attrition

RESOURCE 3.2
The Coastal System

RESOURCE 3.1
The effects of weathering, coastal processes and human activity on the coastline

Rivers bring eroded material from the land to the sea

Weathering processes
Physical Biological Chemical

Up and down

EROSION → Material (sand, shingle + pebble) → TRANSPORTATION → DEPOSITION

Hydraulic Corrasion Attrition Solution
action

Longshore drift

Coastal Processes

COASTAL EROSION

There are a number of processes by which the sea can erode the land:

Hydraulic Action

When air is trapped in a crack in a cliff by the sheer force of a wave, there is an increase in pressure which will break off pieces of rock.

Attrition

When material eroded from cliffs breaks down into smaller pieces by colliding with other eroded material.

Corrasion

When waves throw sand, shingle and pebbles at a cliff and wear it away.

Solution

When certain rock types (e.g. chalk) react with the sea, which is a weak acid.

NON-COASTAL EROSION PROCESSES

The land can also be eroded by non-coastal processes. These include:

Weathering – When the cliff is attacked by the weather.

a) **Physical weathering**
   Hot weather and frost action both help to create cracks in the soil and rock, which breaks into smaller pieces.

b) **Biological weathering**
   When burrowing animals (e.g. moles, rabbits, worms) and plant roots (trees, grasses, scrubs) disturb the soil leaving it more prone to the physical weathering processes.

c) **Chemical weathering**
   Rainwater is slightly acidic and can dissolve certain rocks (e.g. chalk.)

Human activity

When building takes place on cliff tops or when beach material is removed an increase in erosion may take place.

What factors affect the rate of erosion?

The size of the wave

Waves are usually formed by the wind. The size of a wave depends upon the strength and length of time the wind has been blowing and the distance of sea which the wind has to cross – **the fetch**. Resource 3.3 shows the different fetches affecting the coasts of Norfolk. A northerly wind will produce large waves because the fetch is 4100 km, whereas an easterly wind will produce smaller waves because the fetch is only 220 km.

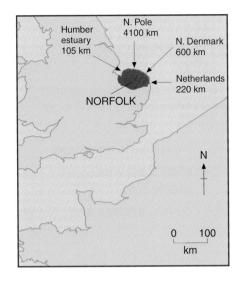

RESOURCE 3.3
The distances waves have to travel to the coastline of Norfolk, UK

RESOURCE 3.4
Clay and chalk cliffs, Norfolk, UK

The hardness of the cliff rocks

RESOURCE 3.5
Granite cliffs, Land's End, Cornwall, UK

Hard, impermeable rocks are more resistant to attack by waves than softer rocks which break up more easily. In Norfolk, erosion of the soft, permeable clay and chalk cliffs can be over 2 m a year. Whereas, erosion of the hard, impermeable granite cliffs of Land's End, Cornwall is 0.001 m a year (Resources 3.4 and 3.5).

25. What are the three processes which shape coastal landforms? Use Resource 3.1.

26. Using Resource 3.2, describe and explain how wave action and weathering processes can erode the coast.

27. What is the fetch of a wave?

28. Using Resource 3.3 and an atlas, calculate the length of fetch (km) of waves approaching the coast of Cornwall from the following directions:

   a) South   **c)** South west

   b) South east   **d)** North west.

29. From which direction is the fetch greatest and shortest?

30. Which area of coast is likely to be affected by the shortest waves? Why?

31. Name the rock types in Resources 3.4 and 3.5.

32. Why are soft rocks more prone to erosion than hard rock types?

33. Why are rock type and weathering processes important in landform development?

What distinctive coastal landforms are produced by erosional processes?

RESOURCE 3.6
Mother Ivey's Bay and Trevose Head (land) near Padstow, Cornwall, UK

There are three main groups of **landforms** which result from erosion by the sea.

- **headlands and bays**
- **cliffs and wave cut platforms**
- **caves, arches and stacks.**

Headlands and bays

These are usually found in areas of changing hard and soft rock. The softer rock experiences most erosion and develops into a bay, leaving the harder rock as a **headland** (Resource 3.6).

Cliffs, wave cut notches and platforms

A **cliff** is a high and steep rock face along a coastline that develops as a result of the erosional action of the sea. At the base of the cliff a **wave cut notch** is formed. As the cliff retreats, a gently sloping rock surface, known as a **wave cut platform** is left (Resources 3.7 and 3.8).

RESOURCE 3.7
Cliffs and wave cut platform, Widemouth Bay, Cornwall

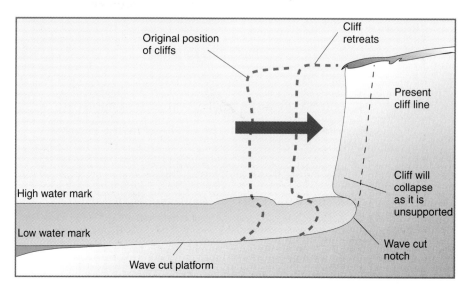

RESOURCE 3.8
How a cliff retreats to form a wave cut platform

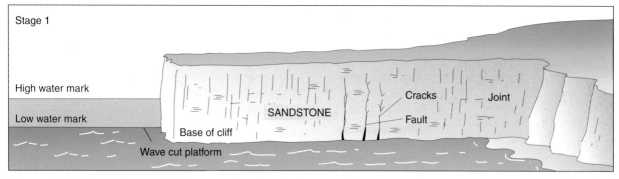

Stage 1

High water mark

Low water mark

SANDSTONE

Cracks   Joint

Fault

Base of cliff

Wave cut platform

The sea attacks between Low and High water mark and erodes the areas of
weathering cracks, joints, faults.

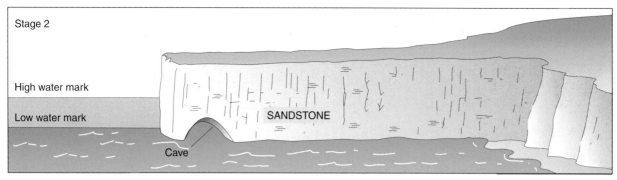

Stage 2

High water mark

Low water mark

SANDSTONE

Cave

Cracks at the base of the cliff get larger and develops
into a small cave.

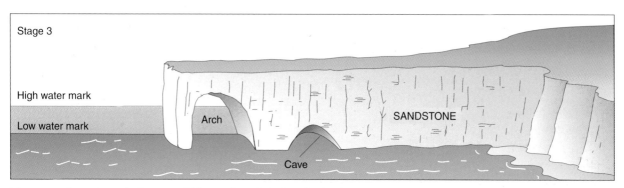

Stage 3

High water mark

Low water mark

Arch

SANDSTONE

Cave

The sea continues to erode the cave which cuts through the headland to form an
arch. Other caves develop.

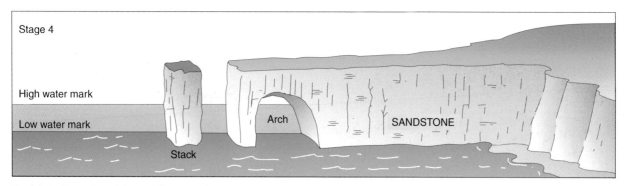

Stage 4

High water mark

Low water mark

Arch

SANDSTONE

Stack

Further under cutting of the arch between the low and high water mark causes the arch to collapse. A
stack is formed, and further undercutting causes the stack to collapse–a stump is formed.

RESOURCE 3.9 A four stage erosion sequence to produce caves, arches and stacks

Caves, arches and stacks

These landforms are formed in headlands, in areas of weakness, such as cracks and joints. Resource 3.9 shows a four stage sequence. The sea attacks a weakness to form a cave, then an arch forms when it cuts right through. Once the unsupported arch collapses, an isolated rock, known as a stack, is formed (Resource 3.10).

RESOURCE 3.10
Stacks in Cornwall

34. Using Resources 3.6 to 3.9, describe and explain how the following landforms are formed:

   a) Headlands and bays.

   b) Cliffs, wave cut notches and platforms.

   c) Caves, arches and stacks.

35. Using Resource 3.10, sketch the landforms and add labels by answering the questions below:

   a) What type of rock forms the headland?

   b) What landforms have been created?

   c) How are the landforms created?

   d) What erosional processes are involved?

   e) What might happen to the landforms in the future?

How does wave action transport material?

The sea can transport material in two ways:

- **up and down the beach**
- **along a beach by longshore drift.**

Up and down the beach

When winds blow at right angles to the coastline, waves will move eroded material up (**swash**) and down (**backwash**) to form a beach.

Along a beach by longshore drift

Waves may break onto a beach at an angle which is less than 90 degrees. When this happens, the waves will move material up the beach at the same angle as they strike it (swash). The backwash returns at right angles to the sea. The result is that beach material gradually moves along the shoreline in a zig zag fashion.

Resource 3.11 illustrates how these two processes create a shingle beach.

36. Describe how wave action transports material.

37. What is longshore drift?

38. Using Resource 3.11, draw a diagram to explain the process.

39. How could you prove the process was happening?

How are distinctive coastal landforms created by depositional processes?

Material eroded from the cliff at one place, will be transported along the coast and deposited to form new landforms. These include:

Beaches

Beaches are one of the most common depositional landforms along the coastline. There are over 300 in Cornwall alone. Material of different sizes can be deposited. Coarser, larger material (shingle and pebbles) is usually carried to the top of a beach, whereas finer material (sand) is found at the bottom (Resource 3.11).

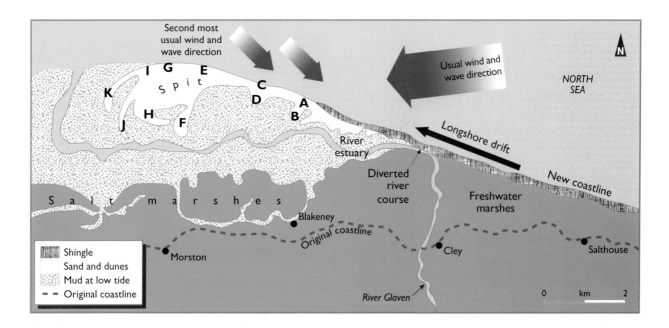

RESOURCE 3.12
How Blakeney Spit, Norfolk is being formed

Spits

A spit is a long area of sand and shingle that grows out across a bay or the mouth of a river. Blakeney Spit, on the North Norfolk coastline, is one of many examples to be found along the coastline. Resource 3.12 shows how a typical spit is formed. Beach material is carried westwards by longshore drift by the usual wind and wave direction, and deposited during calmer conditions (A) forming a spit. The ends of the spit will curve when winds and waves come from a second direction to move the material inland (B). When the winds and waves return to their usual direction, the spit will continue to grow (C). During periods of changed wind and wave directions more curves or hooked ends will develop (D). This process continues E–F, G–H, I–J and K. The spit has diverted the river's entry to the sea along the coast due to its growth. **Sand dunes** develop when the winds pick up sand from the spit, whereas **salt marshes** develop in the sheltered waters behind the spit.

Bars

If a spit develops and grows across a sheltered bay a bar is formed and the coastline is straightened. Water becomes trapped behind and collects in lakes or lagoons (Resource 3.13).

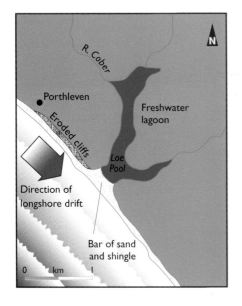

RESOURCE 3.13
How Loe Bar, Cornwall is being formed

Can rises in sea level affect landforms?

Sea levels can rise when ice caps melt due to climate change. A large rise can create a new landform, known as a **ria**, when a river valley reaching the sea becomes drowned (Resource 3.14). A small rise in sea level due to **Global Warming** may drown many low lying coastal landforms, e.g. spits in Norfolk and deltas in Bangladesh and the Netherlands.

RESOURCE 3.14
A ria, Helford River, Cornwall formed due to a sea level rise

40. Define the terms beach, spit and bar.

41. Using Resources 3.11, 3.12 and 3.13, describe and explain how a beach, spit and bar are formed.

42. Where on the coastline would you find a spit and a bar?

43. Name one place in Britain where you would find a spit and a bar.

44. Which coastal landforms are under threat from a future sea level rise? Explain why.

CLIFF COLLAPSE

Key Ideas

There are many causes and effects of cliff collapse.
People respond to and seek to control the hazard in different ways.

Where is cliff collapse taking place in the UK?

RESOURCE 4.1a
The Tees–Exe line

River Tees

N

Older harder rocks

Younger softer rocks

River Exe

The 11 000 km length of coastline around Britain is under constant threat from wave erosion and hence cliff collapse. Some areas experience more cliff collapse than other areas. The Tees–Exe line (Resource 4.1) is an imaginary line running from the River Tees to the River Exe which divides Britain into areas of hard and soft rocks. To the north and west are old, hard, resistant rocks, such as granite and to the south and east are younger, softer rocks, such as clay and chalk. It is the coastline to the south and east of the Tees–Exe line that experiences the greatest cliff collapse.

RESOURCE 4.1c
Mappleton, Holderness coastline, Humberside

RESOURCE 4.1b
Holbeck Hall, Scarborough, Yorkshire

Usually experiences 0.09 m of cliff collapse a year.

Holbeck Hall Hotel collapsed in 1993

Usually experience 2 metres of cliff collapse a year.

RESOURCE 4.1d
Overstrand, Norfolk

45 m lost in 1994 in one fall

Usually experiences 2/3 metres a year of cliff collapse on average a year.

0.3 m a year. Major collapse in 1915.

RESOURCE 4.1e Folkestone, Kent

Answer the following questions using Resource 4.1.

1. What is the Tees–Exe line?

2. Which areas experience the greatest cliff collapse?

3. Why do these areas experience the greatest cliff collapse?

The Norfolk coast

WHAT ARE THE CAUSES OF CLIFF COLLAPSE ON THE NORFOLK COASTLINE?

The cliffs along the Norfolk coastline are made of soft clays and sands, which are easily eroded by the strong waves of the North Sea.

Apart from wave erosion, weathering processes also contribute to cliff collapse. Most cliff collapse occurs during and after prolonged periods of heavy rainfall when water seeps into the land surface. It saturates the sand and lubricates the junction between the sand and the underlying clay. This causes landslides and slumping, movement under the effect of gravity, to take place. Resource 4.2 shows how cliff collapse has occurred along the north Norfolk coastline at various times. Slumping takes place along a slide surface (Resource 4.3 stage 1) and the material slides onto the beach to form the 'toe' (stage 2). Over time this 'toe' is removed by the sea as waves erode the base of the cliff (stage 3). Smaller slides can also occur above the main landslide (stage 4) which will leave a steep sided cliff face. Weathering processes loosen more material and the process continues.

RESOURCE 4.2
Cliff collapse, east of Overstrand on the Norfolk coastline

4. What processes cause cliff collapse on the Norfolk coastline?

5. Using Resource 4.2, describe the cliff collapse pictured.

6. Using Resource 4.3, describe and explain the processes that cause cliff collapse.

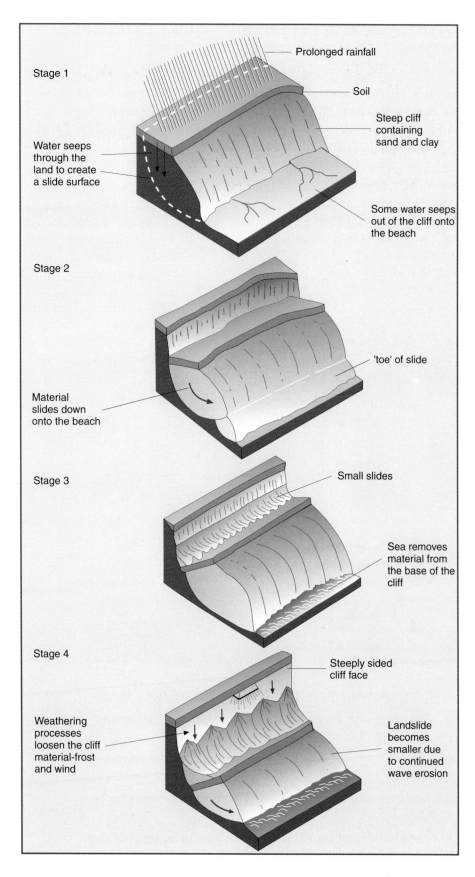

Stage 1

Prolonged rainfall

Soil

Steep cliff containing sand and clay

Water seeps through the land to create a slide surface

Some water seeps out of the cliff onto the beach

Stage 2

'toe' of slide

Material slides down onto the beach

Stage 3

Small slides

Sea removes material from the base of the cliff

Stage 4

Steeply sided cliff face

Weathering processes loosen the cliff material-frost and wind

Landslide becomes smaller due to continued wave erosion

RESOURCE 4.3
The four stages of cliff collapse on the Norfolk coastline

WHAT ARE THE EFFECTS OF CLIFF COLLAPSE ALONG THE NORFOLK COASTLINE?

Cliff collapse along the Norfolk coastline is not just a recent process. History books state that at least ten settlements have been claimed by the sea. The most famous village lost was Eccles which had 80 houses. Others include Whimpwell, Keswick, Foulness and Shipden, which were all lost in the 1300s. The effects of cliff collapse for the people who live and work along the coastline are greater today than they have ever been (Resource 4.4).

RESOURCE 4.4
The effects of cliff collapse on the Norfolk coastline

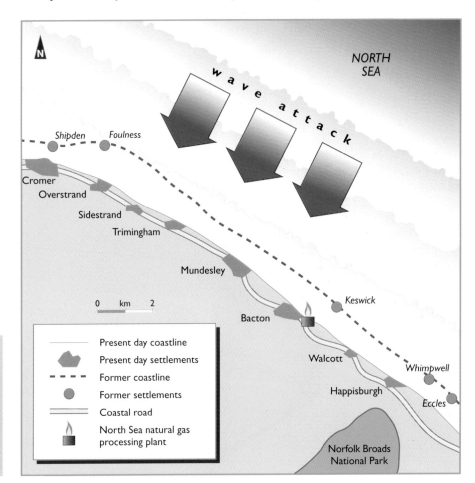

Population (1994)	
Cromer:	7500
Overstrand:	900
Trimingham:	350
Mundesley:	2360
Bacton:	1000
Walcott:	900
Happisburgh:	1200

Cliff collapse as a hazard, includes the loss and damage to:

- **housing** – in Overstrand 30 houses were threatened in 1994, due to a 45 m cliff collapse;
- **schools** – in Sidestrand, two football pitches have been lost in the last 15 years;
- **old buildings** – in Trimingham, the mediaeval church is threatened;
- **tourism** – in Mundesley, hotels, guest houses, holiday chalets and caravan parks are threatened, as well as golf courses around the area;
- **industry** – in Bacton, a natural gas processing plant is at risk;

- **farming** – near Walcott, one farmer has lost five acres of land in recent years;
- **people** – at least 15 000 people live between Cromer and Happisburgh (Resources 4.4 and 4.5);
- **communications** – the coastal road between Cromer and Happisburgh is threatened;
- **Sites of Special Scientific Interest** – the Norfolk cliffs are of environmental interest. At Happisburgh there is also a risk that cliff collapse could threaten the Norfolk Broads National Park in the future.

RESOURCE 4.5
Waves bring end in sight for this home of the brave.

Couple sit tight as waves threaten

Fearless pensioners George and Joan Scott watched the television and drank their tea last night as waves relentlessly pounded their clifftop bungalow.

They had seen it all before, and the worst was over – until the next high tides at 9am today.

The couple, from Beach Road, Happisburgh, are just inches from seeing their retirement home plunge over the cliffs. Decades-old sea defences have been reduced to rubble, and the merciless sea has been let loose to prey on the defenceless cliffs below their home.

But, despite being offered emergency bed and breakfast accommodation for the night by officers from North Norfolk District Council, Mr and Mrs Scott were determined to see it through to the bitter end.

Mrs Scott said: "We signed a disclaimer to say that we are staying here of our own volition, and we don't regret it.

"I'm superstitious, and worry that if we leave for one night, the whole house will be gone when we get back. We've got past the point of worrying."

The couple have been told that if they are concerned at any time they can call 999, and police will come and take them to safety.

THE SCOTTS' DIARY
This is what happened to George and Jean Scott yesterday, as they waited for their house to tumble over the cliffs.

7.52am – woken by television cameraman – who is given a flea in his ear for calling so early.
8am – get up and have a cup of tea.
9.26am – feed the cat and the chickens, and survey Monday night's damage.
10.30am – Anglia TV crew call round.
11.10am – hearty fry-up for breakfast/lunch.
11.30am – BBC Radio Norfolk pop in.
11.47am – Mrs Scott in tears when council officers come round and tell her her three pet pugs may have to go into kennels.

12.45pm – Mr Scott tunes in to hear his wife on the radio.
2.30pm – council officers ring to say they can look at two bungalows, one at Barney, near Fakenham, and one at East Runton.
3pm – tea and biscuits.
5.32pm – feed the dogs.
6.30pm – have a cheese sandwich for tea. Mrs Scott said: "We normally decide what we are going to eat early in the morning, but it's been such chaos we haven't had the time."
7pm – settle down for Emmerdale and The Bill, and listen to the high tide building up.
After 10pm – go to bed, prepared for another restless night.

ON THE BRINK: George and Jean Scott, Happisburgh.

Use Resource 4.4 to answer the following questions:

7. What evidence shows that cliff collapse is not a recent process?

8. What effects has cliff collapse had in recent times?

9. How could human activity be threatened in the future?

Use Resource 4.5 to complete tasks 10 to 14

10. Describe what is happening at Happisburgh.

11. Explain why the couple have to move home.

12. Describe how the couple are coping with the situation.

13. What finally happened to the couple's home?

14. Describe how you would feel if you lived in the same street as the couple.

RESOURCE 4.6
Different methods of controlling the cliff collapse hazard

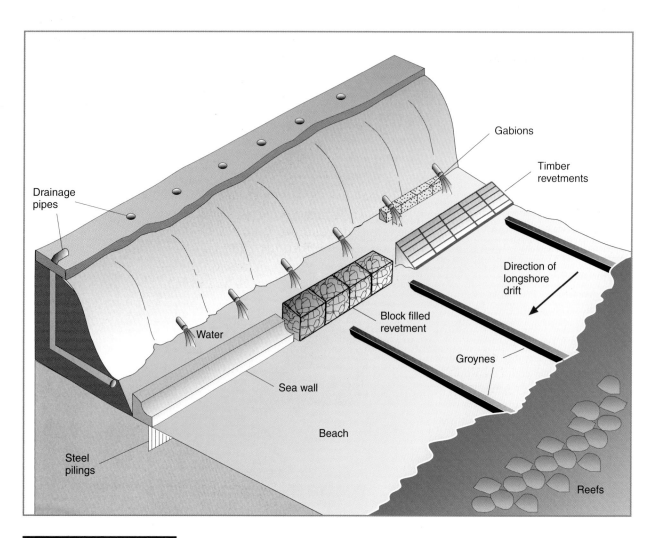

HOW DO PEOPLE RESPOND TO AND SEEK TO CONTROL THE CLIFF COLLAPSE HAZARD?

Three methods are used along the Norfolk coastline to control the rate of cliff collapse (Resource 4.6). These include:

Cliff face solutions

a) **Drainage pipes** – this involves installing pipes through the cliff to the beach below to reduce the amount of rainwater stored and the development of a slide surface.

Cliff base solutions

a) **Sea walls** – a sea wall (Resource 4.7) reflects the energy of a wave, as it is built of concrete. The reflected energy creates erosion in front of the wall, so steel pilings are used to protect the foundations. The cost is £7000 a metre.

b) **Revetments** – there are two types, timber and block filled. Timber types (Resource 4.8) are sloped with timber and have spaces to allow the sea to pass through and over. As a result a beach develops behind which protects the base of the cliff. Timber revetments cost £2000 a metre and are built parallel to the coastline. A block filled type (Resource 4.9) is usually filled with rocks and acts in a similar way to a sea wall.

RESOURCE 4.7
Sea wall and groynes

c) **Groynes** – a groyne (Resources 4.7, 4.8 and 4.9) is a low wall built out into the sea to slow down the transportation of material along the coast (longshore drift). Groynes act as barriers to allow deposition to take place, and cost between £10 000 and £30 000 each.

RESOURCE 4.8
Timber revetment and groynes

d) **Gabions** – gabions are steel wire mesh baskets which are placed at the base of the cliff to give stability. They cost £350 a metre (Resource 4.10).

Offshore solutions

a) **Beach nourishment** – This involves transporting material from other areas to improve the level of a beach (Resource 4.11). This beach material acts as a barrier between the sea and the cliff. This costs £800 a metre.

b) **Reef building** – Reefs are positioned 250 metres from and parallel to the cliff edge. They cause the waves to break early, thus reducing their strength and effect on the cliff edge (Resources 4.12 and 4.13).

How a reef is constructed

The reefs are situated 250 metres from the sea-wall parallel to the shoreline. They are 245 metres long and 45 metres wide and consist of three layers of Swedish granite.

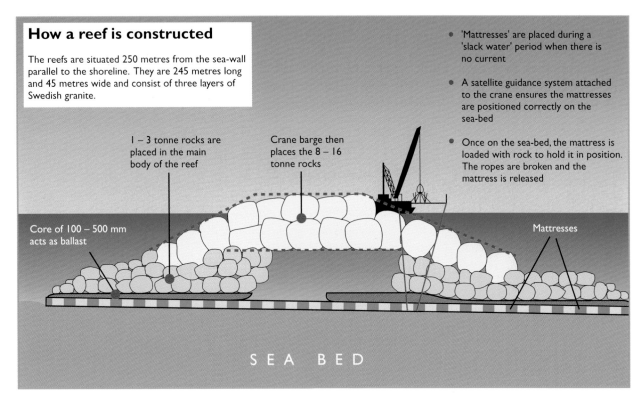

1 – 3 tonne rocks are placed in the main body of the reef

Crane barge then places the 8 – 16 tonne rocks

Core of 100 – 500 mm acts as ballast

Mattresses

- 'Mattresses' are placed during a 'slack water' period when there is no current

- A satellite guidance system attached to the crane ensures the mattresses are positioned correctly on the sea-bed

- Once on the sea-bed, the mattress is loaded with rock to hold it in position. The ropes are broken and the mattress is released

SEA BED

RESOURCE 4.12
How a reef is constructed

RESOURCE 4.13
Reefs

15. Using Resource 4.6, describe the different methods of controlling cliff collapse.

16. Using Resources 4.7, 4.8 and 4.9, describe how sea walls and revetments reduce cliff erosion.

17. Using Resource 4.12, describe how a reef is constructed.

18. Using Resources 4.6 to 4.13, construct a table, similar to the one shown below, to describe the advantages and disadvantages of each form of sea defence.

Defence	Advantages	Disadvantages
Sea walls		
Timber revetments		
Block filled revetments		
Groynes		
Beach nourishment		
Reefs		

19. Explain why sea defences are necessary along the Norfolk coast? Use the answers from Question 4 to help you.

THE CLIFF COLLAPSE HAZARD AT HAPPISBURGH AND THE THREAT TO THE NORFOLK BROADS?

RESOURCE 4.14

Views on the cliff collapse at Happisburgh

People's views or values about what should be done to slow down the rate of cliff collapse at Happisburgh, are varied. See Resource 4.14 below for some of these:

Retired couple

> It is the responsibility of the local government of Norfolk to build sea defences at Happisburgh. The Government cannot afford to build them as there are more important services to provide, like health and education.

Government Minister

> Much of the garden in front of our house has slipped down the cliff and people around us have already lost their homes. New defences should be built to protect people's property. We have a right to live where we wish to.

> Our priority is to protect bigger settlements, like Cromer and Overstrand. The population of Happisburgh is too small (1200 people) to build expensive sea defences.

Local Minister

Professor of Geography

> I have studied the cliffs in this area for many years and I believe nature should take its course. The sea will always win in the end.

> I have been coming to Happisburgh, on holiday for many years now. Over the past 15 years coastal defences have been built, which I believe are ugly and spoil the natural look of the cliffs and beach area.

> We should protect the cliffs at Happisburgh if we are to save the wetlands for future generations to enjoy. The Broads attract thousands of visitors a year and support a varied plant and animal life.

Conservationist

Tourist

Cliff collapse at Happisburgh has become an issue which has made the newspapers (Resource 4.15).

RESOURCE 4.15
Cliff collapse at Happisburgh and the threat to the Norfolk Broads National Park

SEA DEFENCES ■ £4.6 million May Day message to the minister as he inspects county's storm-damaged coastline

By RICHARD BATSON

A home teeters on the edge of oblivion – a stark image that campaigners hope will today shock a Government minister into funding urgent sea defences.

But now a May Day Save-Our-Shoreline message is being sent to the men from the ministry.

Politicians and coastal experts will show junior agriculture minister Tim Boswell that without action now, erosion will cut through ever-weakening sandy cliffs and reach a "point of no return" inside 20 years – swamping the Norfolk Broads, villages and valuable farmland.

Campaigners hope that showing the minister the dramatic reality of the situation at first hand will strengthen their case to cut through Government funding red tape.

MAFF officials have hinted that the Broads threat is not imminent and cannot be brought into play yet as North Norfolk Council tries to justify the cost of a £4.6 million sea defence scheme.

But today's briefing session for Mr Boswell aims to prove that the quickening erosion rate means disaster is getting nearer by the day.

Mr Boswell will see chalets balancing on the edge of cliffs at Happisburgh where erosion has moved into top gear – reaching "speeds" of 13 metres in six months in some places.

Council technical services officer Peter Lawton said it had an excellent case for Government cash.

The technical side of a 100,000 tonne rock defence scheme along a 1300 metre stretch of beach was sound. But the stumbling block was the ministry's insistence that the threat to the Broads was not imminent.

The Government, though it has not formally rejected the scheme, has hinted that the Broads cannot yet be brought into financial equations when assessing the value of land to be saved – which must outweigh the price tag of the scheme under strict cost–benefit rules.

But the council had evidence that rising erosion rates did make the Broads risk an urgent issue.

Investment now in a major scheme would also save public money being spent on trying to repair and maintain shattered existing defences.

Action was needed quickly, and the council was geared up to make a start in the autumn if the government cash became available, said Mr Lawton.

"It is encouraging that he is coming to see for himself. We hope he will see the seriousness of the situation, and hope he responds by relaxing the criteria for releasing money for defences."

A Ministry of Agriculture spokesman said the minister liked to see at first hand areas where there were problems – but his presence was not an indication that the cash might be forthcoming.

There are fears that cliff collapse at Happisburgh will cause the sea to break through and flood the valley down into the Broads.

RESOURCE 4.16
The doorstep of disaster

Responsibility split between authorities

The Government has a simple formula relating to any scheme: the cost of any defence work must be outweighed by the value of what is being protected. Areas of population invariably attract government grant – which can be as high as 75 per cent of the final bill.

But councils find it hard to put forward a successful economic case for protecting less valuable farmland and unpopulated areas.

This is the case at Happisburgh where only part of the proposed scheme would protect homes.

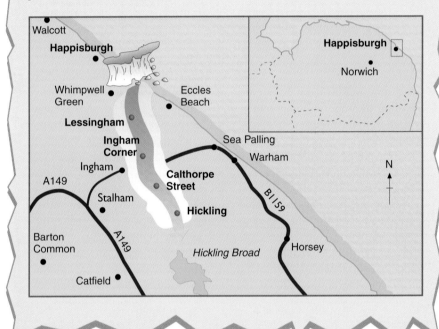

Using Resource 4.14, answer the following questions:

20. Describe and explain who is in favour and who is against protecting Happisburgh from cliff collapse.

21. Why do you think people respond to and seek to control the cliff collapse hazard in different ways?

Using Resource 4.15, answer the following questions:

22. What problem is the sea causing at Happisburgh?

23. Why is erosion so extensive?

24. What might happen to this area in the future?

25. What do people think should happen and why?

26. What do you think should be done and why?

COASTAL FLOODING

Key Idea

Floods are not only caused inland by rain and rivers. Coastal flooding is a problem that has a variety of different responses which are looked at in this chapter.

What are the causes of coastal flooding?

When sea level rises occur above normal levels, low lying areas of the land near the coast will be flooded. There are many causes of abnormal sea level rises. These include:

- under water earthquake activity
- depressions
- tropical cyclones
- high tides
- human activity.

Underwater earthquake activity

Shockwaves from an underwater **earthquake** (Resource 5.1) produce large tidal waves or **tsunamis** which can travel at speeds of 800 km/hr and can be 15 m high.

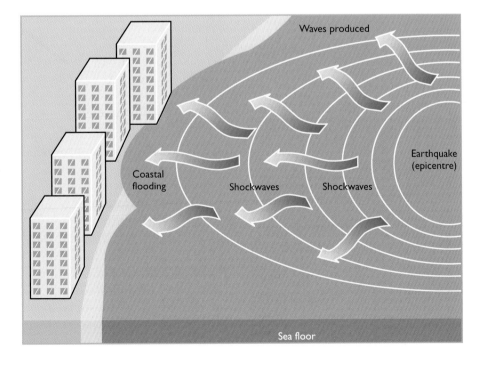

RESOURCE 5.1
Underwater earthquake activity

Depressions

Depressions are huge areas of low pressure. These atmospheric systems measure many hundreds of kilometres across and can be seen on satellite images as masses of swirling cloud. In a depression, air rises so there is less pressure or weight on the sea. As a result, the surface of the sea can rise and waves can push the increased water towards the land to create a **storm surge**. A storm surge is when the level of the sea rises rapidly to a height that was not predicted.

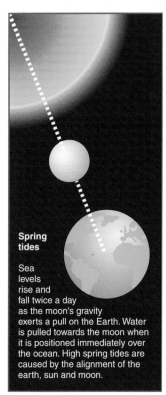

Spring tides

Sea levels rise and fall twice a day as the moon's gravity exerts a pull on the Earth. Water is pulled towards the moon when it is positioned immediately over the ocean. High spring tides are caused by the alignment of the earth, sun and moon.

RESOURCE 5.4
High tides

High tides

Tides rise (**flood**) and fall (**ebb**) twice in 24 hours. This action is caused by a complicated balance between the gravitational effects of the moon and sun, together with the rotation of the earth. The moon pulls water to the side of the earth nearest to it, which creates a high tide. Other areas experience a low tide as water is pushed away. Spring tides occur every month, this is when the tides reach their highest level (Resource 5.4).

PACIFIC OCEAN

RESOURCE 5.3
Satellite image of a tropical cyclone

Tropical cyclones

Tropical cyclones are intense depressions (Resource 5.3). They develop in warm seas (26°C) between latitudes 5° and 20° north and south of the equator. They are known locally as hurricanes (West Indies), typhoons (Asia) or willy-willies (Australia). Like depressions they suck up the sea surface, raising it by 1 to 2 m to create a storm surge.

Human activity

The process by which world temperatures are rising is known as global warming. Human activity is making a major contribution to global warming (Resource 5.5). This includes releasing carbon dioxide into the atmosphere by burning fossil fuels in power stations and by burning tropical rainforests. More heat is trapped, which results in changes in the world climate and a sea level rise due to polar ice caps melting and ice and snow from mountain ranges returning to the sea. CFC gases produced from factories (foam production) and homes (aerosol sprays) destroy the ozone layer in the atmosphere. As a result more of the sun's energy enters the earth, causing global warming to occur.

RESOURCE 5.2
The causes of coastal flooding

Underwater Earthquakes

Most earthquakes are caused by a sudden movement along a fault plane within the interior of the earth. The movement is the result of the release of strain in the rocks that builds up over a period of time. Tsunamis, or seismic sea waves, occur from earthquakes under the oceans, which can travel at speeds of 500 km/hr and can be 15 m high.

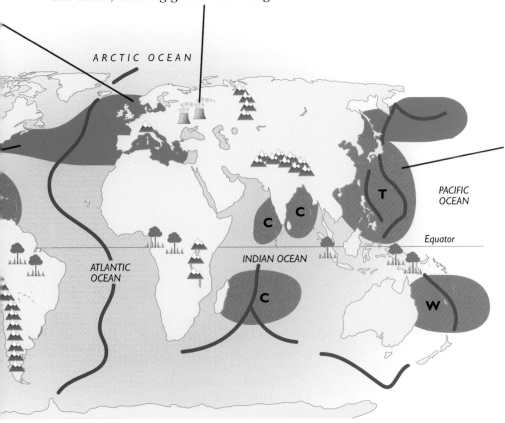

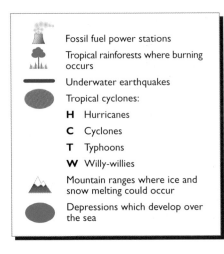

Fossil fuel power stations

Tropical rainforests where burning occurs

Underwater earthquakes

Tropical cyclones:

H Hurricanes

C Cyclones

T Typhoons

W Willy-willies

Mountain ranges where ice and snow melting could occur

Depressions which develop over the sea

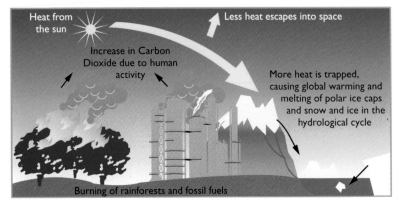

Heat from the sun

Less heat escapes into space

Increase in Carbon Dioxide due to human activity

More heat is trapped, causing global warming and melting of polar ice caps and snow and ice in the hydrological cycle

Burning of rainforests and fossil fuels

RESOURCE 5.5
Human activity

1. Using Resource 5.1 to 5.5, describe and explain the causes of coastal flooding.

2. Using an atlas, identify three areas where coastal flooding is most likely to occur.

3. For each area, explain why the area is at risk from flooding.

What are the effects of coastal flooding?

RESOURCE 5.6

Some effects of coastal flooding around the World

The effects of coastal flooding can be either immediate or of a longer term nature. Tidal waves and storm surges often have a devastating and immediate effect. Whereas a gradual rise in sea level, caused by global warming may seem to have less of an effect, but the results over time could be just as devastating (Resource 5.6).

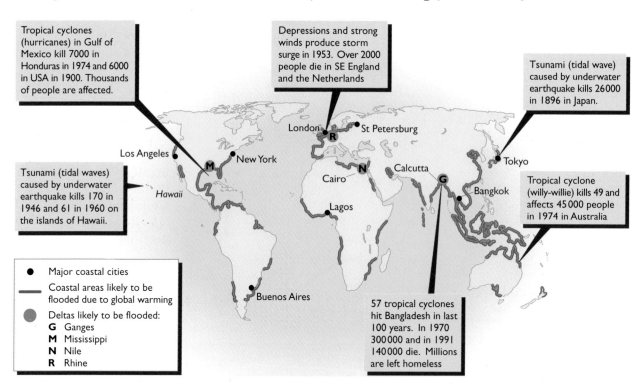

Tropical cyclones (hurricanes) in Gulf of Mexico kill 7000 in Honduras in 1974 and 6000 in USA in 1900. Thousands of people are affected.

Depressions and strong winds produce storm surge in 1953. Over 2000 people die in SE England and the Netherlands

Tsunami (tidal wave) caused by underwater earthquake kills 26000 in 1896 in Japan.

Tsunami (tidal waves) caused by underwater earthquake kills 170 in 1946 and 61 in 1960 on the islands of Hawaii.

Tropical cyclone (willy-willie) kills 49 and affects 45000 people in 1974 in Australia

57 tropical cyclones hit Bangladesh in last 100 years. In 1970 300000 and in 1991 140000 die. Millions are left homeless

London · St Petersburg · Los Angeles · New York · Hawaii · Cairo · Lagos · Calcutta · Tokyo · Bangkok · Buenos Aires

● Major coastal cities
— Coastal areas likely to be flooded due to global warming
● Deltas likely to be flooded:
G Ganges
M Mississippi
N Nile
R Rhine

THE EFFECT OF A TSUNAMI OR TIDAL WAVE ON HAWAII

The worst recorded tsunami on Hawaii occurred in 1946. The rising water flooded a large stretch of low lying coast, with waves 10 m above sea level. Houses floated from their foundations and were swept inland, others were crushed. Many boats were carried inland and damaged. An entire steel span of railway track was ripped loose and carried 300 metres inland. 170 people died and the total cost came to $20 million.

THE EFFECT OF STORM SURGES IN THE NORTH SEA AND THE BAY OF BENGAL

The North Sea

The worst storm surge experienced in the North Sea happened in 1953, when a deep depression formed, which pushed sea water against the North Sea coastline. This happened at the same time as a spring tide and when rivers were flowing into the sea at flood levels. The result was a high tide of between 2 and 2.5 m in South East England and 3 m in the Netherlands. The immediate effect was that 264 people drowned in England and 1835 in the Netherlands. Homes and farmland were under water (Resource 5.7).

The Bay of Bengal

During autumn, tropical cyclones push water northwards up the Bay of Bengal, which becomes narrower and shallower towards Bangladesh, causing storm surges which may be up to 8 m high. The water sweeps over the flat islands of the delta and carries away buildings and any form of life in its path. The record of deaths and damage is almost unbelievable, the worst was in 1970 when 300 000 people were drowned. One person's experience illustrates the effects.

Some other effects are illustrated in Resource 5.8.

RESOURCE 5.8

A storm surge in the Bay of Bengal 1970 produced by a Tropical Cyclone

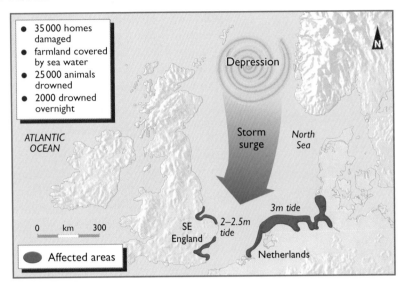

- 35 000 homes damaged
- farmland covered by sea water
- 25 000 animals drowned
- 2000 drowned overnight

ATLANTIC OCEAN

Depression

Storm surge

North Sea

3m tide

2–2.5m tide

SE England

Netherlands

0 km 300

Affected areas

RESOURCE 5.7

Intense depression creates storm surge in the North Sea

Year	Deaths
1963	22 000
1966	80 000
1970	300 000
1985	40 000
1988	25 000
1990	140 000

'At midnight we heard a great roar growing louder from the south east. I looked out. It was pitch black, but in the distance I could see a glow. The glow got nearer and bigger and then I realised it was the crest of a huge wave. I was lucky because I live in a solidly built house and we went upstairs. But thousands were just swept away. The wave came as high as the first floor of my house. We were not poor people on this island but prosperous fishermen and rice farmers. Now we are all street beggars. Everything is gone. All the cattle are dead, all the sheep and goats and most of the buffaloes. All the fishing vessels have been lost and all the nets. We are shy to beg from you, but please, I do beg you to get help for us. We have no drinking water – that we need above all. But we must have vaccines and other medicines too, and we need food.'
Daily Telegraph, November 1970

THE EFFECT OF A SEA LEVEL RISE ON COASTS

A rise in the World's temperatures will result in the melting of the polar ice caps and the ice and snow held on mountain ranges around the World. Melting will increase the flow of water into the sea and lead to an estimated rise in sea level of 0.2 m by the year 2030 and 0.65 m by the year 2100 (Resource 5.6). The effects of this rise will include:

- a threat to the major cities and ports on the coastline;

- loss of valuable farmland for rearing animals and growing crops;

- drowning of the major river deltas of the World – Nile, Mississippi, Rhine and Ganges. A 0.5 m rise in sea level will result in 15 per cent of Bangladesh being under water. A 1.0 m rise would flood 30 per cent of Egypt's farmland and would result in 8 million people leaving the Nile delta;

- some small Pacific and Indian islands would be completely drowned e.g. The Maldives;

- new landforms would be formed e.g. Rias.

Resource 5.9 shows places in Britain which would be threatened due to a rise in sea level. Major cities would face drowning (e.g. Chester, Edinburgh, Exeter, Norwich), valuable farmland would be lost (The Fens) and there would be the loss of wildlife habitats (Norfolk Broads, saltmarshes).

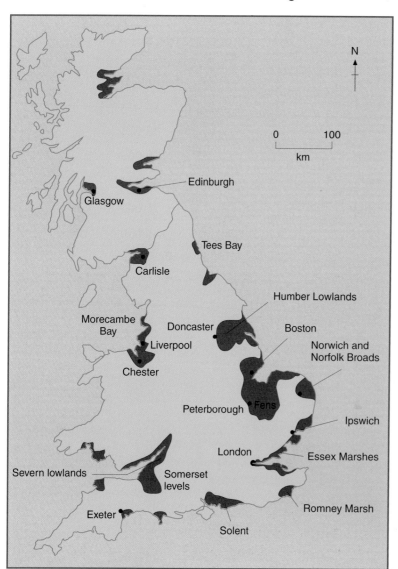

RESOURCE 5.9
Areas of the UK at risk from rising sea levels

4. Using Resource 5.6, list the effects of coastal flooding by Tsunamis and hurricanes.

5. Using Resource 5.7, what effect did the storm surge of 1953 have on South East England and the Netherlands?

6. Using Resource 5.8, what immediate short-term and long-term effects did the storm surge cause in Bangladesh in 1970?

7. Describe and explain why the effects in Bangladesh were worse than in the UK and the Netherlands.

8. Using Resource 5.6 and an atlas, decide which areas of the World are at greatest risk due to a global sea level rise.

9. What would be the likely effect on human activity if this were to happen?

How do people respond to and seek to control coastal flooding?

People respond in many different ways in an effort to try to control and reduce the risk of coastal flooding. Miami, Florida suffers hurricanes on average one every seven years. As no part of the 15 km bar is higher than 3.5 metres above sea level, people have responded by spending £30 million to make Miami beach hurricane proof. The protection scheme includes evacuation routes, a widened beach to create an extra barrier and artificial mounds 6 m above sea level for all new buildings Resource 5.10.

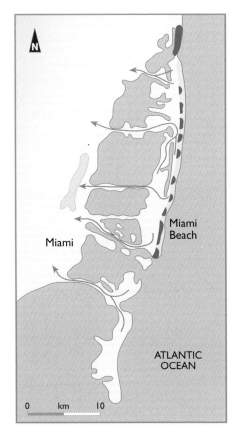

RESOURCE 5.10
Hurricane protection in Miami, Florida

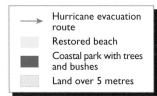

Because most tsunamis are formed by distant earthquakes under the Pacific Ocean, the countries of Japan and Hawaii have developed sensitive recording instruments (**seismographs**) to detect shock waves. As a result time is made available to alert people living on low ground near the coastline and to evacuate them if necessary.

UK RESPONSES TO COASTAL FLOODING

In the UK, the battle to prevent the sea from invading the flat, low lying land in coastal areas began nearly 2000 years ago when the Romans built earth embankments to protect the land they had drained for farming.

Today, the threat is still there and particularly in eastern England where 25 per cent of the region between the Humber and the Thames estuaries is below the highest recorded sea level. 750 000 people and billions of pounds of property and farmland are threatened (57 per cent of grade 1 land is between 0 and 5 m above sea level). The response to coastal flooding has been to:

a) Build sea defences (walls, revetments, offshore reefs) to protect property and communications.

b) Build the Thames Barrier to reduce the flood risk in London Resource 5.11.

c) Monitor beaches and the sea bed along the coastline for areas prone to flooding.

d) Improve wind, wave and sea level monitoring.

e) Renourish beaches with extra material in those areas not protected by sea defences.

f) Provide flood warnings. The Environment Agency issues Yellow (flooding possible), Amber (flooding likely) or Red (serious flooding likely) warnings to the police, who issue public warnings and sound sirens.

However, protection of every kilometre of coast is not financially possible.

RESOURCE 5.11
The Thames Barrier, London

NETHERLANDS' RESPONSE TO COASTAL FLOODING

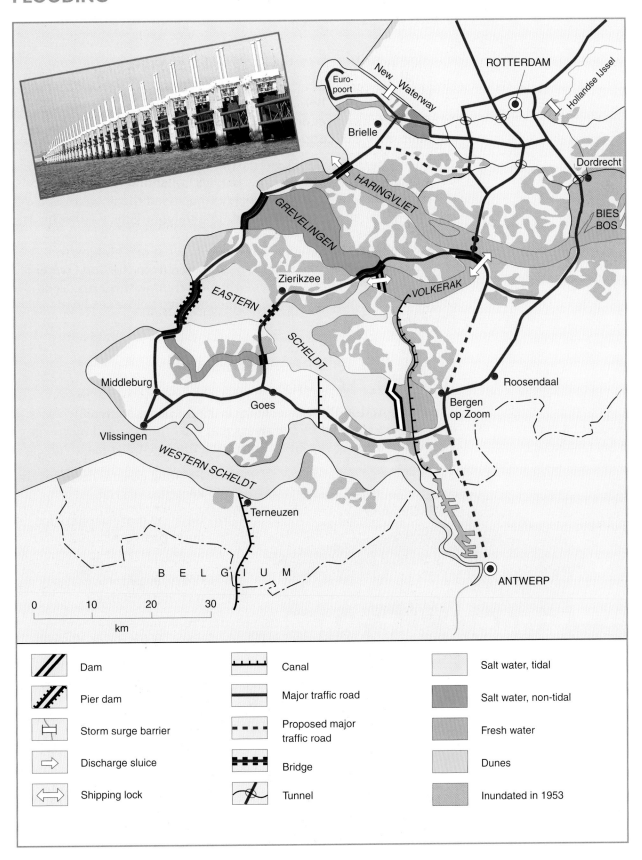

ROTTERDAM

Euro-poort

New Waterway

Hollandse IJssel

Brielle

HARINGVLIET

Dordrecht

GREVELINGEN

BIES BOS

Zierikzee

EASTERN

VOLKERAK

SCHELDT

Middleburg

Goes

Roosendaal

Bergen op Zoom

Vlissingen

WESTERN SCHELDT

Terneuzen

BELGIUM

ANTWERP

0	10	20	30

km

Symbol	Description	Symbol	Description	Symbol	Description
Dam		Canal		Salt water, tidal	
Pier dam		Major traffic road		Salt water, non-tidal	
Storm surge barrier		Proposed major traffic road		Fresh water	
Discharge sluice		Bridge		Dunes	
Shipping lock		Tunnel		Inundated in 1953	

The Netherlands responded to the great flood of 1953 with a huge scheme known as the **Delta Plan**, so that such a disaster could never happen again. The plan aimed to protect the country from coastal flooding by building:

a) Nine dams to reduce the length of the coastline by 700 km, creating 15 000 hectares of new land which was reclaimed from the sea for farming. These areas are called **polders**.

b) A complex system of offshore reefs, embankments and reinforced sand dunes.

c) The Eastern Scheldt Flood Barrier, 3 km in length with 63 movable gates. (The Thames Barrier in London is 500 m long, with 4 movable gates). The barrier balanced the need for coastal protection and conservation of the tidal mudflats, wading birds, fish and oysters.

The Delta Plan was completed in 1986 at a cost of £3 billion to ensure the people of the delta are protected from the flood waters of the North Sea. This is particularly important in this area, as 60 per cent of the population (i.e. 15 million) live below sea level (Resource 5.12).

BANGLADESH'S RESPONSES TO COASTAL FLOODING

RESOURCE 5.13a
A flood shelter

The **Flood Action Plan** was set up in 1989 to help control two sets of floods, one caused by the rivers and the other caused by storm surges and a rising sea level. Protecting the coastal areas involved:

a) Building coastal defences to keep the sea out.

b) Building more shelters for flood protection (Resource 5.13a).

c) Providing improved early warning systems.

d) Preparing emergency services for more effective help after a flood.

In 1993, with sponsorship from the World Bank and the European Union, a dam was built across the mouth of the River Feni, 10 m high and 3000 m long. Twelve million bricks were baked and broken by hand to make the concrete facing. Clay was dug and put into jute bags.

Sand from the river could not be used as it sifted through the bags. Two hundred and fifty thousand tonnes of river rock was transported from northern Bangladesh, as the delta is stoneless. It was a massive human undertaking on what can only be described as a small scale river. Billions of pounds are required to provide defences along the whole coastline, money the country cannot afford (Resource 5.13b).

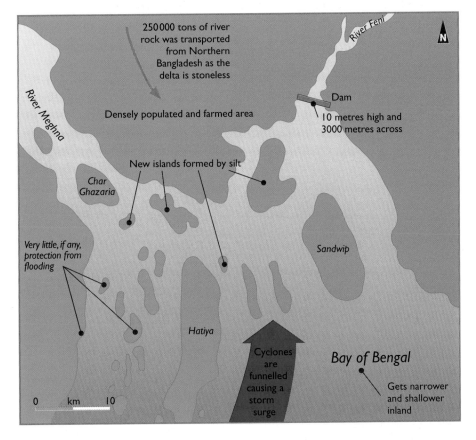

RESOURCE 5.13b
The Flood Action Plan, Bangladesh

10. Using Resource 5.10, describe and explain how people in Miami, Florida, USA, have responded to coastal flooding.

11. Only five bridges connect Miami beach with the mainland and 45 per cent of the population are of retirement age. Explain why these facts might make evacuation difficult.

12. Using Resource 5.11, describe and explain how the UK has responded to coastal flooding.

13. Using Resources 5.12 and 5.13, describe how the people of the Netherlands and Bangladesh have responded to coastal flooding.

14. Explain why the responses to the flood hazard were different.

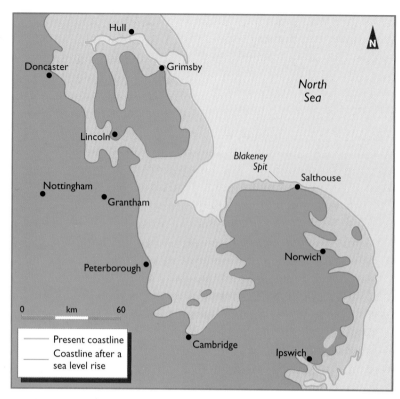

RESOURCE 5.14
How the East Coast might look in the year 2050

The battle to save a village and a nature reserve on the Norfolk coastline.

Fight or flee? This is the decision facing the villagers of Salthouse (population 200), on the Norfolk coastline and conservationists from Cley-Next-The-Sea's nature reserve (Resource 1.24 GR 0743 and 0544). They must decide whether this low lying area should be protected against storm surges and a future sea level rise (Resource 5.14).

The area has been threatened by storm surges on many occasions: 1978, 1983, 1990, 1993 and perhaps most famously by the Great Flood of 1953 (Resource 5.7), when much of the village was destroyed in little under half an hour: 'Dead animals were floating all over us, lovely birds from the nature reserve were dead all around. Personal belongings and furniture lay in the fields and gardens at the back of the wrecked houses. An elderly woman was swept through the window of her kitchen and was later found dead in the back garden. It was a tragedy I will never forget.' A Salthouse resident (EDP newspaper 1953).

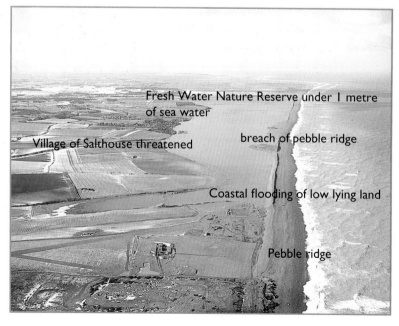

Recently, in 1996, a storm surge swept away the protective pebble ridge and came within metres of the village which had been sandbagged and evacuated earlier (Resource 5.15). Property was not damaged, but the internationally famous fresh water nature reserve (Resource 1.24 GR 0444 and 0544), was flooded with damaging salt sea water.

RESOURCE 5.15
Half a mile inland, sea takes a grim toll

People have responded and sought to control the flood hazard in different ways Resource 5.16.

RESOURCE 5.16
The flood hazard on the Norfolk Coast

Local residents

All we have is a tiny shingle ridge standing between the village and the North Sea. To let the village disappear would be criminal. Better sea defences are needed.

There are a number of possibilities. These include maintaining the pebble ridge, the existing line of defence and reprofiling it at the lowest points with bulldozers. Or we could build new defences offshore by either beach nourishment or reefs. Or else we could abandon the pebble ridge and let the sea develop a salt marsh. This would provide protection for the village by reducing the wave power.

Building expensive sea defences would be wrong for only 200 people, so we should give compensation and ask them to move elsewhere to bigger settlements which have been protected. We should give the freshwater nature reserve back to the sea and let it become a saltwater marsh instead. This would attract even more birds.

Professor of Geography

This is an internationally important nature reserve that is threatened by coastal flooding. It is a 400 acre site which attracts 100 000 people a year in search of identifying Warblers, Terns, Godwits and Bitterns — a rare species. This reserve must be properly protected from the invasion of the salt sea water.

Local council member

Conservationist

RESOURCE 5.17
Bulldozers re-profile the pebble ridge

Location Name: Gramborough Hill Location Number: 1 Grid Reference: 085453 Time: 1.00pm Date: 13/3/97			
Pole No's	Distance (m)	+ −	Angle (°)
1–2	8.3	+	10
2–3	2.4	+	19
3–4	2.7		0
4–5	3.6	+	6
5–6	9.3	+	12
6–7	3.6	+	11
7–8	5	+	27
8–9	7	+	18
9–10	8.8		0
10–11			
11–12			

Location Name: Salthouse Location Number: 2 Grid Reference: 072447 Time: 1.27pm Date: 13/3/97			
Pole No's	Distance (m)	+ −	Angle (°)
1–2	7.9	+	5
2–3	1.5	+	15
3–4	4.65	+	5
4–5	9.67	+	10
5–6	2.5	+	10
6–7	2.9	+	7
7–8	1.7	+	12
8–9	9.6	+	20
9–10	2.9	+	21
10–11	6.65		0
11–12			

Location Name: Arnold's Marsh Location Number: 3 Grid Reference: 059450 Time: 1.50pm Date: 13/3/97			
Pole No's	Distance (m)	+ −	Angle (°)
1–2	9.35	+	7
2–3	0.7	+	16
3–4	4	+	5
4–5	15	+	8
5–6	4.4	+	9
6–7	5.5	+	20
7–8	5.05		0
8–9			
9–10			
10–11			
11–12			

Location Name: Cley Eye Location Number: 4 Grid Reference: 048453 Time: 2.15pm Date: 13/3/97			
Pole No's	Distance (m)	+ −	Angle (°)
1–2	3.9	+	9
2–3	2.1	+	4
3–4	0.7	+	5
4–5	2.8	+	10
5–6	9.1	+	9
6–7	4.1	+	8
7–8	5.3	+	7
8–9	12.1	+	2.5
9–10	6.3		0
10–11			
11–12			

RESOURCE 5.18

Pebble ridge data for four places: Gramborough Hill, Salthouse, Arnold's Marsh and Cley Eye

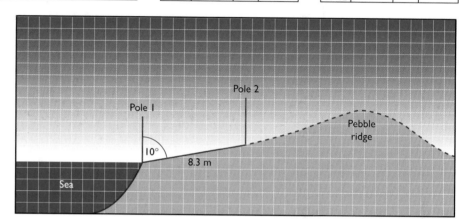

15. Using Resources 1.24, 5.14 and a road atlas, decide which areas and settlements on the east coast, would be threatened by a sea level rise.

16. Using Resource 5.15, describe the effects storm surges have had on the Norfolk coastline.

17. Using Resource 5.16, describe how people wish to control the flood hazard.

18. The short-term solution is to 'fight' the flood hazard by reprofiling the pebble ridge with bulldozers (Resource 5.17). Using Resource 5.18, construct four cross-sections to indicate which of the following places: Gramborough Hill (GR 0845), Salthouse (0744), Arnold's Marsh (0545) and Cley Eye (0445) need immediate reprofiling work to protect the low lying area.

19. The longer-term solution would be to 'flee' the area. Using Resource 5.16, describe and explain who would be for and who would be against the proposal.

20. Why do you think people respond to and seek to control the flood hazard in different ways?